Fi:
for

Edited by Bill Howes

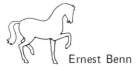

Ernest Benn

Published by
Ernest Benn Limited
25 New Street Square, London, EC4A 3JA
& Sovereign Way, Tonbridge, Kent, TN9 1RW

First edition	1955
Second impression	1956
Third impression	1957
Fourth impression	1958
Fifth impression	1959
Sixth impression	1960
Seventh impression	1961
Second edition	1962
Third edition	1963
Second impression	1964
Fourth edition	1965
Fifth edition	1969
Sixth edition	1978

©W.J. Howes 1978
ISBN 0 510-22512-8
Printed in Great Britain

The front cover photograph, by Bill Howes,
shows the River Thames at Windsor

Foreword

Fishing for Londoners began as a somewhat selfish desire on my part to reduce the number of anglers asking me where-to-fish questions. That was in 1953, shortly after *Angling Times* was first published. As the only member of the paper's staff who had had wide experience of fishing in London and the Home Counties it fell to me to answer all queries relating to that area.

There were so many of them, so exasperatingly many, particularly by phone ('I read your paper. Can you tell me what time the barges pass through Ponders End lock on Thursday mornings?'), so I decided to put what I knew of London's fishing into a small book in the hope that it would cut down the volume of correspondence and telephone calls.

The book was published in 1955, a slim little volume of forty-eight pages, at a cost of 2s. 6d. a copy, and from then on, with a straight face and an easy conscience, I could recommend inquiring London anglers to buy a copy of *Fishing for Londoners.*

Keeping up to date with the fast-changing prices of permits, ownership of waters and so on wasn't easy (there were seven impressions and four editions in the first ten years) but it was much easier than answering letters and telephone calls.

But for domiciliary reasons I have fished less and less in the London area in recent years and have thus become less and less capable of keeping the book up to date. I am happy that the publishers accepted my suggestion to hand the task to Bill Howes, whose knowledge of London's angling scene is deeper and wider than that of any person I know.

I'm glad that over a period of twenty years this little book with the self-explanatory if ambiguous title has introduced an ever-growing number of London anglers to new waters. The choice of where to fish is infinitely wider now, and this completely rewritten edition admirably reflects it.

Ken Sutton

Contents

Introduction

This is the sixth edition of *Fishing for Londoners*. It has changed considerably in its lifetime. In this new edition the changes are apparent both in format and in the arrangement of the contents. The page size now conforms with the rest of the titles in the series of Benn Fishing Guides, being smaller than previous editions. The material in the book is now rearranged on a more strictly geographical basis, with The Thames included as the first section; and with sections 2 to 5 devoted to waters in the north west, south west, south east and north east respectively. There is now a double page map to each of the sections, on which appear most of the locations of the waters described. Anglers are advised to use more detailed maps for more precise identification of locations.

Waters have qualified for inclusion where it has been thought that they provide worthwhile fishing for Londoners and are within easy reach of Central London. Generally this means that they are not more than 35 miles from the centre, although we have included some more distant venues which are easy to reach.

In this new edition we include information about the increasing preponderance of syndicate fisheries in the London area, and also include the names and addresses of many tackle dealers in the region.

The editor and publishers would be very pleased if users of this guide would let them know of any additional information which anglers might find helpful, for inclusion in future editions of this book. Please write to Bill Howes, c/o Ernest Benn Limited, 25 New Street Square, London EC4A 3JA.

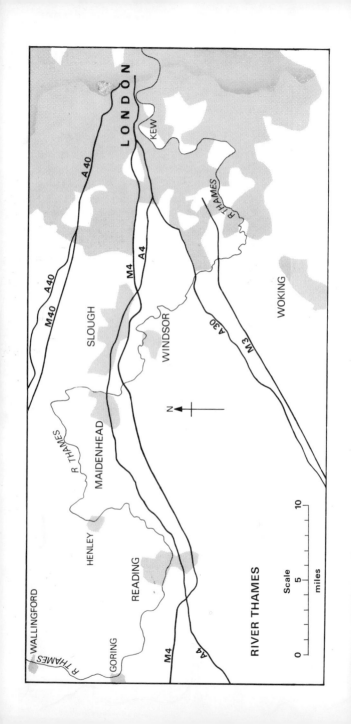

RIVER THAMES

Scale

0   5   10

miles

The syndicates and their waters

The Leisure Sport Angling Club, a subsidiary company of RMC (Feltham), is the largest of the commercially run coarse fisheries syndicates.

Leisure Sport offers fishing on some 43 gravel pit lakes and 11 river stretches on 30 venues in the counties of Surrey, Sussex, Hertfordshire, Essex, Middlesex, Hampshire, Nottinghamshire, Oxfordshire, Norfolk, Kent, Buckinghamshire and Berkshire.

Group and single fishery permits are issued to individual anglers, and there are club arrangements. Permanently pegged match venues are planned for the 1978-79 season.

Leisure Sport have some 15,000 permit-holders, who supply a constant flow of entries to the club's 'Catch of the Month' competition. Permit-holders also have discount facilities at the Leisure Sport Tackle shop and office, at 47-49 Church Street, Staines, Middlesex.

Within a 15 to 25 miles radius of Central London are fisheries of the Boyer's Angling Scheme. This commercial gravel company has eight lakes and several river stretches in Middlesex and Buckinghamshire included on a group season permit. There are also single-fishery season permits available. This company's fisheries include some old-established waters, and others noted for producing specimen-size fish. Further details from Angling Manager, William Boyer Fishing, Trout Road, West Drayton, Middlesex.

One of the latest to join the ranks of the commercial fisheries is Redland Sand and Gravel Company. Starting in the 1978-79 season the angling scheme caters for season permit holders, day ticket visitors, and match fishing. The scheme started with established fisheries at 20 venues, and among the first to be included were Denham Lake, Bucks, a stretch of the Thames at Caversham, Berks, stretches of the Lea and the Great Ouse, and a group of pits at St. Neots, Hunts.

Further details from Angling Manager, G. Rowles, 'Lakeview', Old Bury Hill, near Dorking, Surrey.

Although they are not exactly a commercial fishery, a group of waters which are accessible via a useful season permit are the eleven ponds in the Royal Parks. The permit covers the Serpentine Lake as well as ponds in Richmond Park, Bushey Park and the Home Park. Early application is advised to the Superintendent, Hampton Court Gardens, Hampton Court, Middlesex.

One of the greatest value-for-money permits is a membership card of the London Anglers' Association. Known simply as the LAA, its members have fishing on many miles of rivers, canals, and numerous lakes, gravel pits and reservoirs. Most of these waters are within easy reach of London.

Associate membership is open, by application to the Secretary, H.J. Wilson, LAA, 183, Hoe Street, Walthamstow, London E17.

1
River Thames

This first section is devoted to the water which is Britain's largest river, and certainly one of its best all-round coarse fishing rivers. It is also used, in this guide, as the boundary between the northern and southern waters described in the book. We consider fishing on the Thames from Mungewell Park Farm and below.

Thames, River

The Thames is the Londoners' river, and it holds a wide variety of fish making it one of our finest coarse fishing rivers.

It is hoped that in the not too distant future the river will have a run of salmon because a consignment of around 5000 alevins (baby salmon) have been released into the river at Twickenham.

There are shoals of bream, big barbel and chub, numerous dace, bleak, gudgeon, roach, carp, pike, perch, ruffe, eels and — in places — trout and grayling.

The source of the river is at Thames Head, near Cirencester. From there it flows for some 200-odd miles to the estuary well below London, and throughout its length there are numerous opportunities for catching quality fish.

There are TWA weirs which are fishable by holders of a weir permit. This special permit allows fishing in the weir pools all the year round, and most of the pools hold enough trout to make it worthwhile fishing for them. The weirs hold bigger than average fish, particularly barbel, chub and pike. Incidentally, anglers are permitted to use only one rod and line on a weir.

The weir permits, which are valid from January 1 to the end of December, are issued by Thames Water Authority (Conservancy Division), Nugent House, Vastern Road, Reading, RG1 8DB. They permit fishing on 21 weirs, which are situated at the following places, working downstream: Grafton, Radcot, Rushey, Shifford, Eynsham, Sandford, Sutton, Day's, Cleave (upper), Goring, Shiplake, Marsh, Hambleden, Marlow, Bray, Boveney, Romney, Bell, Shepperton, Sunbury and Molesey. There are other weirs on the river, not covered by the permit.

Bath Road PS hold the fishing at Mungewell Park Farm, easily reached via the A329 from Reading. Reserved for members only, so apply to the club secretary, C. Gardner, 8 Lilac Gardens, Ealing, London, W.5. From here downstream to Goring it is the London AA which holds most of the fishing. TWS's Goring Weir lies close to the road bridge, and the fishing in the pool is excellent for chub, barbel, roach, dace, pike and the occasional big trout. The pool is available to weir permit holders.

There is some free fishing on the Oxfordshire bank, below Goring bridge, and the LAA takes over again and controls a long stretch down river through Hartslock Woods.

Ye Olde Thames AC (YOTAC) holds the fishing rights on the opposite bank at Basildon. The bankside meadows downstream to Pangbourne are popular fishing areas, noted for roach, bream and chub. From the YOTAC fishery Mike Stratton of Reading caught a world match record of 175 lb 4½oz of bream in 1977. No day tickets. Membership details from club secretary, G. Hammond (tel: Reading 476799). There is some free fishing from the towpath at Pangbourne Meadows.

At Pangbourne the weir pool, with its attractive backwaters, offers fishing in peaceful surroundings, but a boat is essential to reach the better swims. Boats are usually to be hired from the boatyard by Pangbourne Village.

Whitchurch meadows, access from Pangbourne village, opens up more excellent fishing opportunity with many good bream swims, and some fine roach to be caught, particularly from the National Trust bank.

Mapledurham is a popular reach with extremely good fishing. A monster pike of 28lb was taken a few seasons ago. The LAA have a fine stretch above the lock, and further downstream it is the Elthorne AA who controls the fishing on the opposite bank upstream and downstream of the weir, for members only. Elthorne AA is an amalgamation of five affiliated clubs, and members enjoy good fishing with individuals' catches of quality chub, bream, roach and dace often exceeding 25lb. Further details of membership from the club secretary, C. Wilde, 9 Elmwood, Maidenhead Court Park, Maidenhead, Bucks.

Further downstream the Englefield Green AA have the Chazey Farm fishery, reserved for members only. Membership is open on application to the club secretary, R. Young, 65 Bond Street, Egham, Surrey.

On the opposite (Berkshire) bank there is the Tilehurst stretch of free fishing, where plenty of bream, chub, roach and dace offer the main sport. At the lower end of the Tilehurst stretch lies Caversham Reach, where the fishing from Thameside Promenade is controlled by the local Reading Council. Angling clubs can book the stretch for contests, but it is usually unoccupied on weekdays when individual anglers enjoy the free fishing.

Reading Council also controls the fishing from Christchurch Meadow and Kings Meadow, where excellent mixed catches of roach and dace have been made, including some 2lb-plus roach.

Fishing is free along the towpath bank downstream of Caversham lock, and also below Reading Bridge. It is still free along the Sonning Dreadnought stretch, as far as Sonning Bridge.

On the opposite (Oxfordshire) bank, members of the London AA have an attractive fishery almost opposite the power station intake. LAA members have more fishing from the Sonning Island, between the weir and the road bridge.

Further downriver, near where the tributary River Loddon joins the Thames, some fine chub, barbel, roach and pike are taken. The local Twyford AC has fishing for members, enquiries to the club secretary, D. Metcalfe, Millwood, 10 Ambleside Close, Woodley, Berks.

Shiplake and Binfield Heath AC has a long and exclusive fishery, on the opposite bank. Most Thames species are to be taken here.

Hennerton fishery is a backwater of the Thames at Wargrave, Berks, and the fishing along half a mile of single bank is held by the London AA.

The water offers exclusive fishing for a variety of species, for members of the Association. Membership details from the Secretary, H.J. Wilson, LAA Office, 183 Hoe Street, Walthamstow, London, E17.

Hennerton backwater is reached via the M4, turning off into the A423 Henley road, into the A321 to Wargrave. The entrance to the fishery is marked 'Watersmoon'.

Visiting anglers have an opportunity for free fishing at Henley, where there are fine roach, chub and bream. Near Hambledon Lock there is a day ticket stretch, and the LAA have from Medmenham to Temple Ferry, which has deeps, shallows and streamy runs of a stretch known as Hurley Flats. Bailiffs issue day tickets for a long section.

Marlow AC members have fishing on the Buckinghamshire bank, and visiting anglers must apply to the club secretary, G. Owen, 15 Greenlands, Flackwell Heath, Nr. High Wycombe, Bucks.

Downstream of Wootton's boathouse is the Bourne End stretch and on the Buckinghamshire bank the fishing is held by the LAA for members and associate members only.

One of the most attractive reaches of the Thames is at Cookham and there is free fishing to be had. A short section to Boulter's Lock is controlled by the Maidenhead & District AA (secretary: A. Brocklebank, 39 Francis Way, Slough SL1 5PH), and day tickets are issued along the bank on Monday to Friday — but weekends are reserved for members.

Below Maidenhead railway bridge is the 'Wall' free stretch, and it offers the chance of fine barbel and chub. From here down to Bray Lock there is a fine stretch held by Boyer's Angling Scheme. For details of season permits apply to Boyer's, West Drayton, Middlesex.

The noted Dorney Reach holds excellent chub and barbel, and there are roach, dace, bleak and gudgeon to make the weights. The fishing rights of this 2 miles long fishery downstream to Boveney Church are held by Maidenhead & District AA who issue day tickets, from Monday to Friday. The fishery provides enjoyable sport to anglers using float methods, and the blockend-feeder/leger style usually finds plenty of barbel in most of the swims throughout the reach.

One main restriction is that keepnets are not allowed, the only exception to this rule being its relaxation in bona fide matches.

Below the Boveney Church the LAA issue day tickets for the single bank section downstream to Cuckoo Bridge. From this small footbridge along the Clewer Meadow down to the motorway bridge, and including the backwater, is controlled by the Salt Hill AS. Day tickets are issued by club bailiffs. Plenty of fish are to be caught here, with a few bream to 9lb, plus chub and barbel. Salt Hill AS secretary is M. Hughes, 42 Cruise Road, Cippenham, Slough, Bucks.

Along the Brocas Meadow it is free fishing and therefore popular at weekends. There is a council car park convenient to the river.

The Thames now reaches Windsor, where it is overshadowed by the castle. There is more fishing below Windsor road bridge. The island separating Romney Lock Cutting from the main stream below the weir is a popular stretch, holding all the usual species. Day tickets are issued by Old Windsor AC bailiffs. Club secretary is R. Kent, 15 Bond Street, Englefield Green, Surrey.

Downstream of the lock cut to the railway bridge is held by Kingsmoor Anglers for members only – apply to club chairman, W.A. Dick, 5 Wharfs Road, Wraysbury, near Staines, Middlesex. There is a free stretch of the river down to Victoria Bridge that fishes well. Below Albert Bridge there is a day ticket stretch above the towpath bank that is controlled by the local Old Windsor club. At the downstream end of the club stretch is a long lock cut that offers useful free fishing, especially in winter, when the main river is in flood.

Continuing downstream, the river reaches Runny-mede, and this is free fishing throughout the reach. Roach and dace fishing is good from the National Trust bank.

Steeped in history this Trust property includes land on which the Magna Carta was signed, and here the Magna Carta and John F. Kennedy memorial stones are situated. There is good fishing in the river for most species.

In keeping with other reaches of the Thames the

roach revival is in evidence, with catches of quality roach totalling 20lb and more, and including several fish of around a pound, with the occasional 1½-pounder.

Below Runnymede the fishing is free from all accessible banks. From Bell Weir to Staines Bridge the fishing along the south bank includes swims by the gasworks, and these are noted for barbel to 10lb, carp up to 24lb, and occasional big chub.

Downstream of Staines Bridge the towpath switches to the opposite bank, and the free fishing continues downstream to Penton Hook Lock. Below the lock the river extends down through Laleham to Chertsey Bridge, and the swims along this part of the river provide excellent sport with barbel, chub, bream, roach and dace.

From Walton bridge there is access to Shepperton Island, where the fishing is still free, and there is the Desborough Channel, average fishing, but useful in winter when the main river is at flood level. Walton is a very popular fishing spot with ample swims, a variety of species, and a large bankside car park by the bridge.

A Thames backwater at Sunbury that is noted for fine catches of barbel, chub, roach, and other species, is held by the Feltham PS. The fishing is reserved for members of the club, and details of membership are available from the secretary R. Sharman, 36 Sandy Way, Walton, Surey.

The towpath extends through Sunbury and Hampton Court, and then switches to the opposite bank, below Hampton Court Bridge. Barbel are a particular quarry here, yet it is mainly dace and roach that provide much of the sport. At Kingston Bridge the fishing again switches to the opposite bank, and Canbury Gardens, Kingston is a popular match fishing stretch.

Good roach fishing is to be found above the Teddington reach and it is here that the last weir on the river is situated. Downstream of the weir the river is tidal, and it holds mainly roach, dace, gudgeon, bleak and some bream.

Richmond is the most popular fishing stretch of the tidal Thames. Without doubt the dace in this area are of the finest quality to be found almost anywhere along this great river.

Along the Surrey bank, Richmond, is a noted match fishing venue, and the ideal centre for this reach is Ham car park. The venue extends upstream to Teddington Lock and downstream to the locks just below Richmond bridge.

It is this lower section of the venue that is most noted for big dace, with 20lb plus totals of sizeable fish always a possibility. In addition to dace there are quality roach, and fish of 2lb have been taken.

Access to the river is fairly easy at several points, with the Ham car park reached from the Richmond to Kingston road.

The river at Isleworth, easily reached from London, has provided anglers with catches of bream and some fine carp. The river here also holds roach, dace and bleak, and ruffe to provide good general sport. Further down at Kew some fair catches of roach and dace have been taken, particularly from the bank alongside the Botanical Gardens. From here on the river travels through the heavily built-up area of London, and it is seldom fished.

Below London the river flows towards its estuary, and the species to be encountered include bass, mullet, smelt and flounder, as well as the occasional freshwater fish. Regular surveys made between 1964 and 1977 have established that around 90 different species of fish have been taken from the river between Fulham and Northfleet.

Tackle dealers

Cookes, 69 Northumberland Avenue, Reading, Berks
(tel: Reading 82216)
Cycles and Tackle, 29 Bridge Street, Walton, Surrey
(tel: Walton 21424)
Gillouds, 1 Old Crown, Slough, Bucks.
Morgan's, 17 High Street, Hampton Wick, Kingston, Surrey
(tel: 977 6013)
Reading Aquarist, 64 King's Road, Reading, Berks (tel: Reading 53632)
Slough Sports Centre, 245 Farnham Road, Slough, Bucks
(tel: Slough 21055)
J. Smith, 4 High Street, Maidenhead, Berks (tel: Maidenhead 21038)

Thurston's, 360 Richmond Road, Twickenham, Middx (tel: 892 4175

Tulls Supplies, 258 Kentwood Hill, Tilehurst, Reading, Berks (tel: Reading 28249)

Turners, 211 Whitley Street, Reading, Berks (tel: Reading 84361)

Windsor Angling Centre, 157 St. Leonards Road, Windsor, Berks (tel: Windsor 67210)

Wyer's, Oxford Road, Reading, Berks (tel: Reading 55614)

Wyer's, 93 Southampton Street, Reading, Berks (tel: Reading 82304)

2
North West

All waters described in this section lie to the north of the River Thames. The eastern limit is the River Lea, which is dealt with in section 5.

The A4 Pit

There is a large ex-gravel pit lake at Colnbrook, Bucks. that is particularly noted for big tench. Fish up to 8lb have been reported, and there have been numerous 6-pounders. Most of these big tench have been caught laying-on with break flake, and a sweet corn bait.

The lake is adjacent to the A4 Colnbrook By-Pass, and it is controlled by the Queen Victoria AS. There are no day tickets, but for membership apply to R. Mathews, 15 Alexandra Road, Hounslow, Middx.

Aldenham Reservoir

Located in the pleasant Hertfordshire countryside, the Aldenham Reservoir at Elstree is easily reached from Watford (A41 then A411). This fairly large reservoir, with natural banks, is owned by Hertfordshire County Council, and has yielded some fine catches of fish in recent years, particularly pike. It also holds bream, tench, and roach. Day tickets issued at the reservoir.

Ashmere Trout Fishery

A well established trout fishery at Shepperton, Middlesex consists of two lakes of 15 acres and 4½ acres. Access is via Felix Lane, near the start of the M3 and about 18 miles from Central London.

The original lake of the fishery, known as Ashmere, is very atractively landscaped with weeping willows and bankside shrubs, and contains wily trout to interest the angler. This is not a day ticket fishery, and a permit is issued for a full season's fishing. It is a beautiful and secluded water, so it is not surprising that there is always a waiting list for permits.

The second lake is a more recent development but pleasantly landscaped nevertheless. It is of some 15 acres, first opened as a trout fishery in 1970, and the average weight of trout taken is estimated at around 1lb 9oz, which means some fairly big fish are also taken. Fishery records are: brown 6lb 14oz, and rainbow 8lb. There are a couple of boats, plus plenty of bank space.

A full season permit allows a member to fish at any time from March 15 to September 30. There is also what is known as a half-season permit, which allows a member to fish on any three set days. For instance, on a Monday, Thursday and Saturday, or on a Tuesday, Friday and Sunday.

This fishery is run by Mr and Mrs K. Howman, of 'Ashmere', Felix Lane, Shepperton, Middx (tel: Walton 25445).

Bedfont Lake

A water which could be holding specimens is Bedfont Lake. It has all the usual stillwater species and, in fact, in the past it has produced roach to 2½lb, pike to 24lb, and carp to over 20lb.

The lake is situated in Bedfont, Middx, and access is via Clockhouse Lane, reached from the A30 Staines to Bedfont road, turning into Clockhouse Lane at the junction with A315. At the other end of Clockhouse Lane is the B377 Feltham road. There is a fairly large car park close to the water.

There are no day tickets issued. Season permits are issued by the Angling Manager, Leisure Sport, RMC House, High Street, Feltham, Middx.

Blenheim Lake

Blenheim, the home of the Duke of Marlborough at Woodstock in Oxfordshire, is set in surroundings that are very pleasant and peaceful.

Always the roach are worth fishing for, and there are some very big fish. For the specimen hunter there are two-pounders, and a good shoal may be located almost anywhere around the lake. Float-fishing with bread on a size 12 hook, fishing it just off the bottom, is often the best way — and there is no mistaking the bites.

A popular species on this water is the tench, and bags of 100lb have been taken in recent seasons. Of course the best tench fishing time is during the early weeks of the season, and it is during this time that catches will almost certainly include fish around the 5lb mark.

In winter visiting anglers are usually more interested in the pike fishing, with fish over 10lb fairly common, and 20-pounders a possibility.

Blenheim Palace, with its lake and acres of woodland, is a popular tourist attraction. There is no bank fishing at Blenheim, so the angler has to hire one of the boats, which must be booked in advance. To check the price and availability, ring the Estate Office (tel: Woodstock 811432).

Bowyer's Pit

A well established ex-gravel pit lake of about 4 acres, set in the Lea Valley at Cheshunt, Herts. There is some bankside vegetation, and the swims average 5ft to 6ft close in, shelving to aroung 20 ft close in, shelving to around 20ft in places.

Stock includes carp, tench, bream and pike. The lake is noted for its pike fishing, with plenty of fish in the 20lb to 25lb range. Spinning and dead-baiting are the favourite methods on this water.

Controlled by the Duke of Wellington AS for season permit holders. Permits are issued by T. Huckstep (Tackle), 123 Fulbourne Road, Walthamstow, London, E17 (tel: 527 1135).

The fishery is reached via Hertford Road to Theobalds Grove Station, turn into Trinity Lane, cross the railway and turn left to the entrance. There is a large car parking area.

Boxers Lake

A popular coarse fishing water in Enfield, Middx with access from Lonsdale Drive, controlled by the Borough of Edmonton. The lake holds roach, bream and other

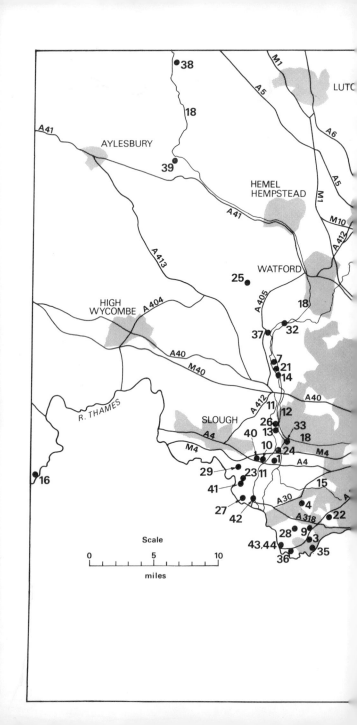

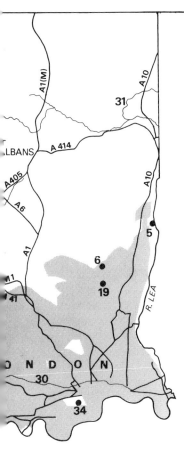

NORTH WEST

1 A4 Pit
2 Aldenham Res.
3 Ashmere Trout Fishery
4 Bedfont Lake
5 Bowyers' Pit
6 Boxers Lake
7 Broadwater Pit
8 Bushy Park
9 Charlton Pit
10 Colnbrook Fishery
11 Colnbrook River
12 River Colne
13 Cowley Lake
14 Denham Lake
15 Duke of Northumberland River
16 Folley's Pit
17 Frogmore Pits
18 Grand Union Canal
19 Grovelands Lake
20 Hampton Court
21 Harefield Lake
22 Kempton Park West
23 Kingsmead Fishery
24 Larbourne Farm
25 Latimer Park
26 Little Britain Lake
27 Longfield Lakes
28 Q. Mary Res.
29 Q. Mother Res.
30 Regent's Canal
31 River Rib
32 Rickmansworth A'drome
33 Rodney Meadow
34 The Serpentine
35 Shepperton Fishery
36 Sheepwalk Lake
37 Springwell Lake
38 Tiddenfoot Pit
39 Tring Reservoirs
40 Willow Pool
41 Wraysbury No 1
42 Yeoveney Fishery
43 Littleton Lake
44 Taywood Lakes

species. Day tickets are issued at the lakeside, and juniors' permits are at a reduced rate. Season permits on application to Borough Treasurer, Civic Centre, Silver Street, Enfield.

Broadwater Pit

This large lake at Harefield, near Denham, Bucks. has a great reputation for holding huge pike. The Gerrards Cross AS hold the fishing rights for members only. The lake has produced pike over 30lb, and in the season 1972-1973 over 23 pike weighing 20lb and over were caught.

Club membership details from D.J. Gates, 2 Leys Close, Harefield. The fishery is reached via Moorhall Road, and lies about one mile from Denham Station.

Bushy Park

In this Royal Park there are three waters — Heron Pond, Diana Fountain Pond and the Leg of Mutton Pond. All these waters hold pike, tench, roach, rudd, perch, common carp and crucian carp.

The Diana is a small ornamental pond, recognizable by the Diana Fountain in its middle, and it is fed directly by the small Longford River. This little pond holds a fair head of fish, including pike of double figure proportions, perch, carp, roach and tench.

The Heron Pond and the Leg of Mutton Pond are connected, and they hold bream, roach, pike, tench, rudd and some carp. Applications to fish these waters should be directed to the Superintendent of Hampton Court Gardens, Hampton Court, East Molesey, Surrey.

Charlton Pit

At Sheepwalk, Shepperton, is a gravel pit owned by the Charlton Sand & Ballast Company, and the fishing is controlled by Staines AS. This old-established water is noted for bream, tench and roach. There are no day tickets. Membership details from the club secretary, G. Brown, 134 Page Road, Bedfont, Middx. (tel: 890 0261).

Claydon Park Lakes

The Top and Middle lakes in Claydon Park near Winslow, Bucks reached via the A413 have become noted for such unusual species as the zander and Danubian Wels catfish. A former British record zander of 8lb was caught from this Claydon Park fishery, and the biggest catfish scaled 33¼lb.

The lakes also hold large common carp, bream, roach and tench. Night fishing is not allowed, and fishing is by season permit issued by the Leighton Buzzard AC secretary, F.Groom, 29 Albany Road, Leighton Buzzard, Beds.

Colnbrook Fishery

The Colnbrook Fishery, consisting of Lakes Nos 1, 2 and 3, is a part of the Boyer's Angling Scheme. The lakes are situated about 1½ miles west of London's Heathrow Airport, and reached via the A4 road.

Quality fish are caught most seasons, with tench over 5lb, bream over 10lb and a top pike of 32lb from Lake No. 1. The lake also holds carp, roach, rudd and perch. Lake No 2 is the smallest water in the Boyer's scheme yet it holds a fine head of tench, bream and roach. Nearby lies lake No 3, and this popular water also holds a good stock, particularly of carp.

This fishery is reserved for season permit holders, and application must be made direct to William Boyer, Boyer's Angling, Trout Road, West Drayton, Middx (tel: West Drayton 45141).

Colnbrook River

This small but interesting river, fairly shallow with a reasonable flow, holds most of our coarse fish species. In the Colnbrook, Bucks, area the Englefield Green AA holds the fishing rights on a fine stretch of the river. Sport on this club's fishery is mainly with small chub, dace, and roach. Englefield Green AA's stretch of the river runs close to the Colnbrook By-Pass (A4) and the fishery is for members only.

A further stretch of the Colnbrook at Wraysbury,

near Staines, Middx, best reached from the A30, is also held by the Englefield Green AA. From this water members have caught carp, barbel, big chub and roach.

Membership of the Association is open, and applications should be sent to the secretary, R. Young, 65 Bond Street, Egham, Surrey.

Also at Wraysbury, the Blenheim AS holds the rights to a prolific section of this small river. Some fine roach catches are made, and the angler can expect carp, dace, chub and pike (the last up to 20lb).

A surprise catch of a 3lb 2oz golden orfe was made a couple of seasons ago. Three other golden orfe in the 1¼ to 2lb range have since been caught. Membership details from the secretary, C. Cargill, 14 Camden Passage, London N1.

Colne, River

A Thames tributary that flows through Buckinghamshire and Middlesex to join its parent river at Staines.

Most Thames species are to be caught at the confluence of the two rivers, where there are a few productive swims. Working upstream the river flows through Wraysbury and close by the Blenheim club's lakes, and this club holds some fishing for its members. Details of annual membership from the secretary, C. Cargil, 14 Camden Passage, London N1.

At Poyle the river flows well, with shallows and pools, and it holds dace, roach and chub. The Bath Road PS holds the fishing rights, and annual membership is open by application to the secretary Charlie Gardner, 8 Lilac Gardens, Ealing, London W5.

From the old Bath Road at Longford downstream for three-quarters of a mile the fishing is controlled by the Staines AS. Species include roach, dace, gudgeon and small chub. There are no day tickets. Membership details from club secretary G. Brown, 134 Page Road, Bedfont, Middx. (tel: 890 0261).

Englefield Green AA has a fine stretch of this river near Colnbrook, Bucks, and the club's water is adjacent to the A4. The swims here are best fished by float, and the catches comprise chub, dace, and roach. Reserved for members only, details of membership from secretary

Roger Young, 65 Bond Street, Englefield Green, Surrey.

Also at Colnbrook, a seldom fished section of the river, rather overgrown, holds chub, roach, dace, perch and the occasional trout. This is included on a season permit issued by Boyer's Angling, Trout Road, West Drayton, Middx (tel: West Drayton 45141).

Further excellent fishing is to be had in the stretch that runs under the M4. This section is part of the Leisure Sport AC Larbourne Farm fishery at Iver. Season permits only on application to the Angling Manager, Leisure Sport, RMC House, High Street, Feltham, Middx.

Also at Iver, Bucks there is a wide pool below a weir, holding most of the river's species, and this free fishing is enjoyed by local anglers. A nearby public house, The Anglers Retreat, is a useful landmark.

Moving upstream, above Thorney Weir, the river is private to members of the Metropolitan Police AS. But a little further up the river runs alongside the Little Britain lake and is fishable by day ticket issued along the bank. It is easily reached via the lane by the Paddington Packet Boat public house.

Also near here is the Boyer's Farlow Lake fishery, and the adjacent stretch of the Colne is included on the season permit. The stock in this part of the river consists of dace, roach, chub, bream, perch, pike and a few barbel.

Further upstream the Uxbridge Rovers AC hold the fishing rights to a prolific stretch, and some fair weights of mixed fish are taken by members. This stretch is reserved for members only, and application for membership should be made to the club's secretary, D. Boothroyd, 140 Eastcote Lane, South Harrow, Middx.

From here upstream the river is held by angling clubs, and details of membership are available from the Angling Manager, Leisure Sport, RMC House, High Street, Feltham, Middx, and London AA secretary, H. Wilson, 183 Hoe Street, London E17.

Cosgrove Lodge Park

This lodge park of 110 acres at Wolverton, near Stony Stratford, Bucks has been developed as an island holiday centre, catering for many aquatic sports including angling. There are seven lakes and two miles of river fishing on the Great Ouse and the Tove. The waters have been well stocked with carp, pike, bream, roach, rudd, perch and tench.

The park is open for fishing from June 16 to March 14. It is situated within 10 miles of the M1 and to the east of the A5, access via the A508. Day tickets are issued. Further information from proprietor, Cosgrove Lodge, Cosgrove, Wolverton, Bucks (tel: Stony Stratford 3360).

Cowley Lake

A secluded water at Cowley, near West Drayton, Middlesex. This is a fairly large lake, with natural tree-lined banks. Species include tench, carp, roach and pike. Float and leger methods are suitable for this water. Day tickets are issued at the lakeside.

This water lies close to the Little Britain Lake, and access is via Packet Boat Lane, off Cowley Road, and marked by the Paddington Packet Boat public house. The nearest railway station is West Drayton.

Denham Lake

At Denham, Bucks, is the Redland Gravel Company's lake, holding a wide variety of coarse fish, available on day and season permits. This large lake is adjacent to the Moorhall Road, and easily reached from Denham Station. Enquire G. Rowles, 'Lakeview', Old Bury Hill, Westcott, nr. Dorking, Surrey.

Duke of Northumberland River

This is a small and narrow stream in Middlesex. During recent season the fishing on a stretch of this shallow stream in the Bedfont—Hounslow area has been taken over by the Feltham PS, and that club has stocked it with several thousand rudd, roach and crucian carp. Day tickets are issued, and applications should be made to the secretary, R. Sharman, 5 St Albans Avenue, Hanworth, Middx.

Folley's Pit

A large lake of 110 acres situated close to the Thames at Sonning, Folley's Pit is controlled by the Central Association of London & Provincial Angling Clubs.

The water holds a wide variety of coarse fish. Among the specimens that have been caught are pike of 28lb, tench 8lb, and bream of 6lb. Day tickets are issued along the bank by a CALPAC bailiff.

Frogmore Pits

A group of four lakes — ex gravel pits — situated about two miles south of St Albans. The fishing is good, with bream, roach, tench, carp and pike. Roach of 2lb have been taken from this water. The lakes vary in depth from 6ft to 12ft. The fishery also includes a long stretch of the River Ver, which has plenty of roach and dace.

The fishing is controlled by the London AA, and day tickets are issued. The Frogmore Pits fishery is reached from the A5, and entrance is via Hyde Lane.

Grafham Water

Grafham Water, a popular fishery with many London trout anglers, is a 1670 acre reservour, at West Perry, Huntingdonshire, which is reached by travelling about 2m west from the Buckden Roundabout on the A10.

This vast water, first opened for fishing in 1966, has produced trout up to 12lb 5oz, and in 1976 a total catch of 36,273 trout was a fishery record. It is controlled by the Anglian Water Authority, fishing is by fly only from bank and boat, and there is an eight fish catch limit.

Day tickets are issued at the reservoir lodge and there is a reduction for juniors and disabled anglers. Season permits from Area Manager, Anglian Water Authority, West Perry, Hunts. Advance Bookings — tel: Huntingdon 810531.

Grand Union Canal

Convenient for London anglers is the Grand Union Canal waterway, generally easy to fish and easily reached. The canal extends from the Paddington Arm, London, through Stonebridge Park, Greenford to Southall, plus a further section at Osterley. Most of the fishing in these areas is by day ticket, and it is also included on London AA permits. The Greenford length in particular is noted for some fine catches of roach, taken on the usual float-fished baits. Further information on the canal sections, and membership details, from the secretary, London AA, 183 Hoe Street, London E17.

Another section of the canal extending for nearly three miles, from Hayes to West Drayton, is held by the Central Association of London and Provincial Angling Clubs. The fishing is available with annual membership open to any angler, on application to CALPAC's membership secretary, F.W. Newman, 907a Oxford Road, Reading, Berks.

The Slough Arm, a section from West Drayton to Langley, was constructed nearly 100 years ago, and the fishing along a six miles length of most of both banks is controlled by the London AA. Day tickets to cover all of this length are issued along the bank.

This is a rather weedy stretch, but it does offer excellent fishing for tench. There are also bream, roach and perch worth catching, and float fishing is the popular method. There are plenty of access points.

From West Drayton to Uxbridge, and northward as far as Denham Lock, is held by the London AA, and day tickets are issued. This whole length covers at least four miles, and the fishing is from both banks. Access to the bank at any part of this is easy, and for users of public transport the nearest railway stations are West Drayton, Cowley and Uxbridge.

There is a good head of fish throughout, and in recent seasons additional stockings of roach, rudd, tench and carp have been made. Some useful swims are to be found in the area where the River Colne joins the canal.

Reckoned to be one of the best fishing lengths is the six miles stretch of the canal from Denham Lock, Bucks, up to Batchworth Lock, Rickmansworth, Herts. This length is controlled by Blenheim AS, and it has been stocked regularly in recent seasons with tench, roach, rudd, perch and crucian carp. The fishing is available to visiting anglers on day tickets issued along the bank.

There is a reduction for juniors. Open matches are held regularly on this Denham section. Further details of this section and club membership from C. Cargill, Blenheim AS, 14 Camden Passage, London N1.

From Kings Langley through Boxmoor, Berkhampstead and Tring, a distance of some 14 miles, there is first-class roach fishing with catches of thirty fish including specimens over 1lb frequently taken. There are various other species along this length, including tench and bream. The fishing rights are held by the London AA, and reserved for members and associate members.

Membership is open to those who apply to the secretary, H.J. Wilson, London AA, 183 Hoe Street, London E17.

A section of the canal known as the Aylesbury Arm also offers good fishing, and a section of this is held by the Tring Anglers, and a further length by the Aylesbury & District AA. Further details from their respective secretaries, J. Smith, 67 Lower Icknield Way, Marsworth, Tring, Herts or E. Wheeler, 20 Verney Walk, Southcourt, Aylesbury, Bucks.

Coventry & District AA holds the rights to a fine stretch and annual membership to this Association is open to those who apply to the secretary, E.C. Baxter, 15 Boswell Drive, Coventry, West Midlands.

The Coventry Association also has a stretch of canal fishing at Fenny Stratford and at Milton Keynes.

Also holding fishing rights on the Grand Union is the local Bletchley Social Club. The club's fishing is for reasonable sport with bream, tench, roach and dace. There are also pike and some perch. Further information can be obtained by enquiry at local tackle shops.

Anglers visiting the canal at Cheddington can obtain day tickets from Luton AC bailiffs, or from local tackle shops. Further details from Luton AC Secretary: D. Titley, 17 Tancred Road, Luton, Beds. This club has about 12 miles of towpath bank extending through Leighton Buzzard to beyond Stoke Hammond. Day ticket fishing opportunities exist throughout this length, which holds good bream shoals and carp well into double figures.

The canal in this area has been well stocked with several thousand roach by the Leighton Buzzard AC, whose members also enjoy the good fishing this canal length has to offer. Membership details of Leighton Buzzard AC from club secretary F. Groom, 29 Albany Road, Leighton Buzzard, Beds.

There are numerous bridges carrying roads over the canal throughout its length, and access is generally easy from most of these road bridges.

Great Ouse River

Fed by its principal Buckinghamshire tributaries the Ouse, Tove and Claydon Brook, the Ouse flows through five counties before it reaches the sea. Throughout this long waterway there is a wide variety of fish to be caught, including bream, roach, chub, tench, dace, barbel, perch and pike. Among the specimens to be caught are chub of around 6lb, roach to 2lb and bream of 6lb.

An attractive stretch of the river in the Buckinghamshire area, easily reached via the M1 from London, offers good fishing in delightful surroundings. Most of the fishing in this area is controlled by the Buckingham & District AA. These upper reaches of the river are noted for big chub in the 5 to 6lb range plus the occasional roach to 2lb. Further details from S. Smith, 46 Westfields, Buckingham.

In the Wolverton, Bucks, area the fishing is controlled by the Milton Keynes Association. There are fine bream, chub and other species. Secretary: J. Baglee, 14 Flint House, Suffolk Close, Bletchley, Bucks.

Another fine stretch of the river flowing through the Cosgrove Lodge Park offers day ticket fishing for chub, dace, roach etc. Further details may be obtained from the Cosgrove Lodge Park, Wolverton, Bucks. Set in rural surroundings this stretch lies within 10 miles of the M1 and one mile of the A5.

Slightly downstream in the Newport Pagnell, Bucks, area there is more good fishing, easily reached from the M1, for a variety of coarse fish. The local Association holds the fishing rights to about 10 miles and issues permits. Apply to the secretary, F.J. Read, 19 Chicheley Street, Newport Pagnell, Bucks.

Downstream much of the fishing is controlled by the

Leighton Buzzard club, and the Stoke Goldington fishery is reserved for members and their guests (secretary: F. Groom, 29 Albany Road, Leighton Buzzard, Beds.).

The Leighton Buzzard AC also has a fine stretch of the river comprising the Church Farm fishery near Olney, and this extends downstream to Emberton Park. Bream to around 6lb make for good fishing, plus quality roach, dace, chub, and pike. It is available to members of the Leighton Buzzard club, and their guests.

Club members also have the adjoining Tyringham Estate Fishery, a further 1½ miles of good coarse fishing. The stretch of the Ouse flowing close to the Emberton Park is included with the lakes, and day tickets are issued by a park bailiff. There is ample car parking space within the park area.

Fairey's Meadow at Olney, Bucks, is also held by this Leighton Buzzard club. This fishery consists of two meadows where the fishing is mainly for bream, chub and dace. The club also has a further stretch of the river extending from the Emberton Park boundary downstream to the road bridge.

The Birmingham AA has a mile of the river at Olney. This fine stretch is used for contest fishing, and it holds a good head of big bream. Applications for membership of this Association (which has numerous fishing waters on several other rivers) to HQ, 40 Thorpe Street, Birmingham.

Also near Olney is a single bank length of fishing at Harold Lodge Farm, controlled by Leisure Sport AC. The fishery is easily reached from London via the M1 to Newport Pagnell then via the A5130 to Olney.

This stretch is well stocked with chub, bream, pike, roach and dace. Season permits only issued on application to the Angling Manager, Leisure Sport, RMC House, High Street, Feltham, Middx.

Further downstream is the Hill Studd Farm stretch at Sharnbrook, near Bedford. This stretch is noted for its coarse fishing, and is also controlled by the Leighton Buzzard AC.

This club controls other parts of the Ouse, including a mile-long stretch of the river at Renhold, near Bedford, upstream of Willington Lock, and a bank-length of the

Mill Pool, plus a mile-long section of the river flowing through Clifton Reynes, Bucks.

The Bedford AC holds the fishing on a length of the river at Bedford, and permits are issued by a club bailiff. The club also has a fine stretch at Brownham and Oakley (secretary: R. Meads, 155 Marlborough Road, Bedford).

There is a stretch of river flowing through the town of Bedford and for at least a mile downstream where Anglian Water Authority rod licence holders may fish free.

A variety of coarse fish are to be caught from the river at Blunham, controlled by London AA, and this is available to members and associate members.

The London Association also has the fishing from two meadows downstream of Barford Bridge, and this is known as the Poplins Wells Fishery. Other Ouse fisheries in the area held by the London AA are at Roxton and Tempsford.

The Bridge Meadows Fishery at Great Barford, Beds, is also held by the London AA, and this fishery extends from Harford Bridge upstream for about threequarters of a mile to a backwater (secretary: H.J. Wilson, London AA, 183 Hoe Street, London E17).

The local St Neots A & FPS have a fine stretch of fishing around the town bridge and bailiffs issue permits. This water is noted for bream, tench, chub and roach. Good chub are to be caught from under far bank tree-lined swims (secretary: S. Smith, 10 River Terrace, St Neots, Cambs).

London AA controls another fishery, which is in two sections at Brampton, Hunts, and extends from the sluice to River Lane, and one meadow downstream to the railway bridge. Coarse fishing, for members of this big Association, is good.

In the Godmanchester area, and opposite the Portholme Meadow, are the Berry Lane Meadows, and all part of the London AA fishery including the West Meadow Fishery — nearly two miles of excellent fishing.

The London AA's Portholme Fishery is a long reach of the main river and a backstream, and it is a noted coarse fishery with ample access points. Bailiffs issue day tickets along the bank.

The Association also holds fishing rights on about

600 yards of the Ouse at St Ives, Hunts, and it is reserved for members only. At Bluntisham the LAA also has fishing rights for some 1½ miles.

At Littleport, Cambs, the local Littleport AC holds some good fishing water for bream, roach and dace, with day tickets issued at the local Black Horse Inn (secretary: D. Clark, 41 Forehill, Ely, Cambs).

The fishing rights of some 14 miles of the river at Littleport are held by the London AA. The noted Littleport Fishery holds fine shoals of bream. The best angling method for these bream is legering, with swim-feeders and swing-tips often helpful. The fishery includes both banks from Littleport Bridge to Low's Farm, the Ten Mile Bank, and on the east bank from the bridge to Modney Drove at Southery, Norfolk. From here on other local organizations hold the fishing rights to various lengths through to the estuary.

Grovelands Lake

Popular with local anglers is the lake in Grovelands Park, at Bourne Hill, Southgate, London. There is a wide variety of species, including tench, bream, roach, perch and pike.

Day tickets are issued at the lakeside, and juniors permits at reduced rates. Season permits on application to Borough Treasurer, Civic Centre, Silver Street, Enfield. Grovelands Park lies near the North Circular Road.

Hampton Court: Home Park

Home Park, behind Hampton Court Palace, contains five good fishing waters: they are Long Water, Overflow Pool, Rick Pond, Willow Pond and the Wall Pond.

In fact the Overflow is a small pool situated at the lower (and more remote) end of the Long Water, which is some 200 yards long and runs to about 6 ft deep. This water contains roach, rudd, chub, tench and pike.

Rick Pond is generally shallow and holds roach, tench (to 5lb 9oz), pike and some carp. The Willow Pond holds a large head of small tench, plus roach, rudd and some carp.

Season permits to fish these waters are issued by the Superintendent of Hampton Court Gardens, Hampton Court, East Molesey, Surrey.

Harefield Lake

Harefield Lake, at Harefield, Middx, is a large water that holds large fish. Carp over 20lb, bream of 11lb, tench up to 8lb, and perch up to 3lb 12oz have been caught in recent seasons.

There are numbers of medium sized pike, with fish over 20lb taken every season, and at least two over 30lb in recent seasons. Season permits are issued, and juniors under 16 years must be accompanied by an adult.

The lake is reached from Moorhall Road, and lies about one mile from Denham Station. This water is controlled by Boyer's, and for a permit apply to Boyer's Angling, Trout Road, West Drayton, Middx.

Kempton Park West

This reservoir of 19 acres, near Hanworth, Middx, is reached via Sunbury Way. It is stocked with brown and rainbow trout and records for the water are brown 7lb 12oz, and rainbow 7lb 8oz. Fishing is by fly only, (no worming) with a six fish catch limit, four fish to part-day permit holders; bank fishing only. The water is controlled by the Thames Water Authority, and day tickets are issued on site. Juniors under 16 must be accompanied by an adult. Permits in advance from the TWA (Metropolitan Water Division), New River Head, Rosebery Avenue, London, EC1.

Kingsmead Fishery

There are two interconnected lakes at Horton, near Wraysbury, Bucks. The Kingsmead lakes have been fishing well, and in the last few seasons roach and rudd to 2½lb have been taken from both lakes. Other fish caught in 1976/77 included tench of 8lb 2oz (many from 5lb to 7lb), bream 5lb, perch 3lb, pike of 26lb 4oz, and eels of 6lb 3oz.

Access to this Leisure Sport AC fishery is via the A30

to Staines, then B376 from the By-Pass, or else by way of the M4.

Season permits only issued, on application to the Angling Manager, Leisure Sport, RMC House, High Street, Feltham, Middx.

Larbourne Farm Fishery

Larbourne Farm fishery is at Iver, Bucks, and may be reached from the M4 and A4 roads. There are two lakes, one situated to the north of the motorway and one to the south. There is also a stretch of the River Colne that is available to permit holders. Quality fish from the waters include pike 20½lb, tench, bream, perch and roach.

This fishery is controlled by Leisure Sport AC, and season permits are issued. Apply to the Angling Manager, Leisure Sport, RMC House, High Street, Feltham, Middx.

Latimer Park Lakes

Latimer Park Lakes, near Chesham, Bucks, are reached via the B485. Situated some 27 miles from London, this fishery consists of two natural lakes, and a stretch of the River Chess — some 13 acres altogether. Regularly stocked, with brown and rainbow trout to 4lb. Fishing, from bank and boats, is by fly only, with a catch limit of five fish.

Little Britain Lake

A popular fishing water at West Drayton, Middx is the Little Britain Lake, which covers a fairly large area.

The lake has attractive natural banks, and there is a good stock of bream, carp, tench, roach and pike. This water can be fished on a reasonably-priced day ticket or season permit, issued by a bailiff at the lakeside.

The main access to the lake is via Packet Boat Lane, off Cowley Road, and marked by the Paddington Packet Boat public house. The nearest railway station is West Drayton.

Littleton Lake   see page 60

Longfield Lakes

There are three lakes at Longfield, Wraysbury, near Staines, reached from the A30 Staines By-Pass, then the B376. These lakes have a reputation of producing specimen fish, and contain bream, tench, roach and carp of heroic proportions. All three lakes are easily accessible from the car park.

This is a fine general coarse fishery, with bream to 7¾lb, tench 5½lb, roach 3lb, pike 19½lb and carp 22½lb taken. All three lakes are of different character, and all hold quality fish. For the carp angler night fishing is allowed.

This is a Leisure Sport fishery, open to permit holders only. Apply to the Angling Manager, Leisure Sport, RMC House, High Street, Feltham, Middx.

Newport Pagnell

Close to the M1, and easily reached from London, is a large group of gravel pit lakes offering excellent coarse fishing. These waters, some 9 or 10 of them, are well stocked with a variety of species. The fishing is controlled by the local Newport Pagnell Fishing Association, and season permits are available from the secretary, F. Read, 19 Chicheley Street, Newport Pagnell, Bucks.

Oughton Fishery

A small natural lake of about 2 acres, about 2m north of Hitchin, Herts, comprises the Oughton Fishery. About 36 miles from London, the fishery is reached from the A600.

The lake is fed by the River Oughton, and owned by the Burford Trout Farm. Stocked with brown and rainbow trout, the fishing is by fly only. Catch limit four fish. All fish to be retained.

Day and season tickets issued at Burford Ray Lodge, Bedford Road, Hitchin, Herts (tel: Hitchin 52855).

Queen Mary Reservoir

This large reservoir of 435 acres (near Staines) and the

Staines North Reservoir at Staines, Middlesex, are both easily reached via the A30 and A308. These are two man-made reservoirs and they hold a variety of coarse fish, including roach, bream, perch, and big pike. The season extends from June 16 to March 14. These Thames Water Authority reservoirs are controlled by the London AA and day tickets are not issued. Associate member's permit on application to LAA Office, 183 Hoe Street, Walthamstow, London, E17.

Queen Mother Reservoir

This new reservoir of 475 acres, situated near Colnbrook, Bucks, is reached via the M4 and A4. There is a large car park in the reservoir area.

Construction of this 475 acres water took five years, the first stock of 46,000 brown trout was introduced in 1975, and a further consignment of 40,000 rainbows was released ready for the opening of the new fishery in 1976.

The stock in this new popular fishing water consists of fish ranging from 12in. in length to 8lb in weight. A season's tally of 433 trout, a record for the reservoir, was taken by Paul Wightman of Slough during 1977.

This comparatively new reservoir is now regularly stocked with brown and rainbow trout, the aim being to maintain a density of 100 fish per acre.

Fishing is by fly only from boats – there is no bank fishing. Catch limit is six fish, or four fish to part-day permit holders. All rainbow trout caught must be killed and counted in the bag limit. Season: rainbow, March 15 to November 30; brown, April 1 to September 30; from 9am to sunset or 9.40pm, whichever is the earlier.

The water is controlled by the Thames Water Authority. Day tickets, including boat hire, are issued at the recreation centre in the reservoir area, Horton Road, Horton near Colnbrook, Bucks. Permits are only issued to juniors between 8 and 16 years if they are accompanied by an adult.

Regent's Canal

Known as London's Canal, this waterway was constructed in the 1800s. The fishing is far better than may be realised, with most species of coarse fish.

Fishing rights on a 10 miles stretch of towpath from Paddington to Commercial Road, near the Regent's Canal Dock, is controlled by the London AA.

A short section at Little Venice, single bank downstream from the Toll House, is also held by the LAA.

The Association also controls the fishing on a single bank section of the Hertford Union Canal that joins Regent's Canal near Mile End Lock.

Fishing is reserved for members only, and details of membership are available from the Secretary, H.J. Wilson, LAA Office, 183 Hoe Street, Walthamstow, London, E17.

Rib, River

This interesting river in Hertfordshire, with varying depths, holds trout, chub, roach and dace. The trout are worth fishing for, with a recorded specimen of 4lb. The fishery is situated at Downfield Farm, Watton Road, near Ware, and may be reached via B158 and B1001.

Season permits are issued by Leisure Sport AC. Apply to the Angling Manager, Leisure Sport, RMC House, High Street, Feltham, Middx.

Rickmansworth Aquadrome

There are two lakes at this venue, known as Batchworth and Bury. The popular fishing water is Batchworth Lake, irregularly shaped and covering some 80 acres. It is well stocked with a wide variety of species, and among the quality fish recorded are pike 20lb, bream 6lb and tench 5lb. There are big carp in this water.

The banks are comfortable to fish from, and there are boats for hire. Day tickets are issued on site. Fishing times are: summer, 9am to 8.30pm; and winter 9am to dusk.

The Aquadrome, at Rickmansworth, Herts, can be reached from the A412 Uxbridge Road.

Rodney Meadow

A good all round fishery is Rodney Meadow, situated about half a mile from West Drayton, Middx. The entrance to the site is on the left just before the railway bridge. Some big nets of average sized tench, although fish of 6lb are caught.

The lake also holds pike of 20lb and over, plus bream, roach, rudd, eeels, common and mirror carp. This lake is also reputed to hold silver bream, with fish of record size. There is a large car park, and West Drayton is the nearest railway station.

The water is owned and controlled by Boyer's Angling, and applications for season tickets should be sent to the company at Trout Road, West Drayton, Middx.

Roxton Park Fishery

This landscaped reservoir of some 15 acres is run as a trout fishery, stocked with brown and rainbow trout. Fishing is by fly only, no hooks larger than size 10 allowed. Season: May 1 to October 31, from 9.30am to one hour after sunset. Both bank and boat fishing are available to season ticket holders. For details of permits apply to the owners, P.C. Bath Ltd, Roxton Park, Beds. (tel: Bedford 870385).

This fishery is situated at Roxton, near Bedford, and is about 50 miles from London via the A1.

The Serpentine

In the Serpentine Lake, Hyde Park, fishing is restricted to certain areas because of boating and swimming, yet the sport can be good. Float-fished breadflake always account for a net of roach. No doubt the reason bread is an effective bait is because the large number of resident ducks are regularly fed on it by the many visitors. The lake also holds bream, carp and perch — and old records show that the lake once produced a 13lb barbel!

A season permit can be obtained on application to the Superintendent of Hyde Park, London.

Shepperton Fishery

At Shepperton, and close to the Thames near Walton Bridge, are two lakes belonging to Leisure Sport AC and known as the Shepperton Fishery. The fishing areas are in two sections.

This water has some great bream, but a shoal has to be located. Recorded specimens are bream 5½lb, tench 6lb, roach 2½lb, perch 2½lb, eel 6lb and pike 25lb. There are plenty of average-sized pike, and several around 20lb reported.

Access is by way of Felix Lane, off the A375 Fordbridge Road, Shepperton. Immediately after turning into Felix Lane the entrance is on the right, where there is ample car parking space.

Season permits only issued, apply to the Angling Manager, Leisure Sport, RMC House, High Street, Feltham, Middx.

Sheepwalk Lake

This is a large ex-gravel pit situated in Chertsey Road, Shepperton (once known as Shepperton Range Pit). The stock includes large bream, plus roach, tench and pike. The fishing is controlled by the Feltham PS, for members only. Membership details from R. Sharman, 36 Sandy Way, Walton, Surrey.

Springwell Lake

This old-established water, controlled by the London AA, holds a wide variety of species including carp, tench, bream, roach, perch and pike. Some extremely good quality fish are caught from this water every season.

Springwell Lake is reached via the A40 to Denham, onto the A412, and into Springwell Lane for access to the fishery. Day tickets not issued. Membership applications to H.J. Wilson, Secretary, LAA Office, 183 Hoe Street, London, E17.

Taywood Lakes see page 65

Tiddenfoot Pit

This is a noted carp fishing lake, near Leighton Buzzard, Beds, controlled by the local Leighton Buzzard AC. In addition to carp (over 30lb), the lake holds tench and Danubian wels catfish. No day tickets. Season permits from Leighton Buzzard AC secretary, F. Groom, 29 Albany Road, Leighton Buzzard, Beds.

Tring Reservoir

There are three reservoirs at Tring, Hertfordshire, known as Startops End, Wilestone and Marsworth, and the fishery is reached via A41 and M1. Fishing is for quality coarse fish with bream recorded at over 12lb, and roach up to 3lb. Wilstone produced a record catfish of 43½lb, and pike over 30lb. Fishing is from bank and boats, and the season is June 16 to March 15. Day tickets and evening permits are issued. There are reduced rates for juniors under 14, and for permits and punt hire consult the reservoir keeper.

Willow Pool

Willow Pool, near Slough, Bucks, is a 10 acre lake noted for big carp. This ex-gravel pit was excavated about 1920, and in recent years it has been well stocked. Season permits only issued, and juniors under 16 must be accompanied by an adult.

Owned and controlled by Boyer's Angling, and applications to the company at Trout Road, West Drayton, Middx (tel: West Drayton 45141).

Woburn Park

Woburn Park has several, generally shallow, lakes that are spring fed and hold a variety of coarse fish. The park is easily reached from the M1, and the A50 turning on to the Ampthill Road which runs through the Woburn Park. The lakes are well stocked with carp, bream, tench, roach, pike and the unusual zander and catfish.

Day tickets are issued, with reduced rates for juniors, O.A.P.'s and registered disabled. There are ample car parking areas. Further details from Bedford Estates, Woburn Park, Woburn, Milton Keynes (tel: Woburn 202).

Wraysbury No 1

This is one of the top fisheries of Leisure Sport AC, and is situated near Staines, Middlesex. Access is via Welley Road, the B476 from the A30.

This Wraysbury Fishery consists of two inter-connected lakes. Well landscaped, they are known as South Lake and North Lake and they cover about 150 acres. This is a real specimen hunters' water. Usually the water is gin clear, with a prolific weed growth, and it holds big fish.

A top haul of 200lb of tench and bream was taken a few seasons ago. Other specimens reported include roach to 2lb 12oz, tench to 7lb 1oz, bream of 9lb 2oz, pike over 25lb, eels to 4lb, and there are some fine carp.

This is not an easy venue to fish because of its size and the clarity of the water. Night fishing is allowed.

There are three entrances, each with car parking areas. Season permits issued, apply to the Angling Manager, Leisure Sport, RMC House, High Street, Feltham, Middx.

Yeoveney Fishery

At Staines, Middlesex, is the Leisure Sport AC Yeoveney Lake, and this holds good fish. The lake is studded with small islands, and is of irregular depth, yet it holds good quality fish.

Of the few reports which have been received there have been catches of carp to around 21lb, tench of 6lb 4oz, bream 8½lb, rudd 2lb 6oz, crucian carp 2½lb, and catches of large numbers of tench are not uncommon. Night fishing is allowed.

Fishing is by season permit, and full details are available from the Angling Manager, Leisure Sport, RMC House, High Street, Feltham, Middx.

Tackle dealers

The Anglers' Den, 474 Lady Margaret Road, Southall, Middx
(tel: 578 2293)

Angling Centre, 265 Bath Road, Hounslow, Middx (tel: 570
6156)

W. Bass, 57 High Street, Feltham, Middx (tel: 890 4616)

Benwoods, 60 Church Street, Edgware Road, London NW8
(tel: 723 9970)

Birch & Son, 207 Royal College Street, London NW1 (tel: 485
9087)

Don's of Edmonton, 239 Fore Street, Edmonton, London N18
(tel: 807 5396)

Farrer's Tackle and Sports, 709 Seven Sisters Road, South
Tottenham, London N15 (tel: 800 3618)

Frames, 202 West Hendon Broadway, London NW9 (tel: 202
0264)

J. Frost, 43 Western Road, Southall, Middx (tel: 571 5153)

Harding's, 239 High Road, Willesden, London NW10 (tel: 459
6661)

J.T. Hunt (Aquapets), 12 Springbridge Road, Ealing, London W5
(tel: 567 3259)

Judds, 3 Westbourne Parade, Uxbridge Road, Hillingdon, Middx
(tel: 573 0196)

Kempston Sports, 1 High Street, Kempston, Beds
(tel: Kempston 854744)

T. Linders, 82 North Street, Leighton Buzzard, Beds
(tel: Leighton Buzzard 2416)

McDonalds, 40 Eastcote Lane, South Harrow, Middx (tel: 422
4375)

Metcalf & Son, High Street, Tring, Herts (tel: Tring 3144)

Patone Sports, 1 Woodthorpe Road, Ashford, Middx
(tel: Ashford 45199)

Pets & Angling, 96-98 Walton Road, East Molesey, Surrey
(tel: 979 9083)

Queensway Pets & Angling, 52 Queensway, Hemel Hempstead,
Herts (tel: Hemel Hempstead 54723)

Sharp's, 162 Maldon Road, London NW5 (tel: 485 1759

E. & J. Smith, 264 Desborough Road, High Wycombe, Bucks
(tel: High Wycombe 27975)

The Sports Centre, 14a Woburn Street, Ampthill, Beds
(tel: Ampthill 403469)

Sports & Fashion, 51 High Street, Huntingdon, Cambs
(tel: Huntingdon 0480)

Stanobs, 982 Harrow Road, Kensal Green, London NW10
(tel: 969 1142)

K. Storer, 123 Feltham Road, Ashford, Middx (tel: Ashford 52443)

Tackle Carrier, 157 St. Albans Road, Watford, Herts (tel: Watford 32393)

Tamesis Tackle, 127 Crossbrook Street, Cheshunt, Herts

Thames Angling, 11 Feltham Road, Ashford, Middx (tel: Ashford 43185)

Tooke's, 311 Ruislip Road East, Greenford, Middx. (tel: 578 2614)

Tooke's, 614 Fulham Road, London SW6 (tel: 736 1484)

Ward's, 70 West Street, Dunstable, Beds (tel: Dunstable 61398)

Watford Supply Yard, 405 Whippendall Road, Watford, Herts (tel: Watford 34952)

Willets, High Street, Newport Pagnell, Bucks (tel: Newport Pagnell 611025)

Woody's of Wembley, 565 High Road, Wembley, Middx (tel: 902 7217)

Young's, 76 Station Road, Harrow, Middx (tel: 427 0119)

3
South West

All waters contained in this section lie to the south of
the River Thames and to the west of the M23/A23
roads.

The A30 pond

Situated on Yateley Common, Hants is the A30 pond.
Noted for its big fish, the pond has produced carp of
22lb, pike over 21lb, plus quality tench, bream, roach
and perch. This all-round water is fishable on day ticket
issued along the bank by a ranger. Juniors and OAPs pay
a reduced charge. Fishing is allowed from 8am to 8pm.

Access to the water is from the A30 Camberley to
Basingstoke road. There is ample car parking in a sign
posted picnic area.

Ameys Pit

A vast lake near Reading offers excellent stillwater
fishing, mainly to members of Reading & District AA.
This Association holds the rights to most of the bank,
and the fishing is for bream up to 6lb, tench to 7lb,
roach 2lb 6oz, crucian carp 3lb 8oz, plus bleak, etc.

Club contests held on this water generally need
double figure catches to win. The fishing is for members
only; apply to the club secretary, F. Newman, 907a
Oxford Road, Reading, Berks.

The lake is easily reached from the A4,

Argents Mere

At Newbury, Berks, the Twickenham PS hold the fishing
rights to a lake known as Argents Mere. This is a popular
venue for club members, who catch crucian carp, tench,
and rudd. Membership is open to those who apply, and
it also covers fishing on the nearby Kennet, and other
waters to the west of London (secretary: Mrs G.

Etherington, 49 Muswell Park Crescent, Hounslow, Middx).

Ash Vale Fishery

Ash Vale Fishery, at Ash Vale, near Aldershot, Hants, is reached from the M3, via the A30 and A3013, turning into Lakeside Road to the fishery. This lake is included on the Leisure Sport AC permit, and holds a variety of species, including roach and tench.

There are no day tickets, but season permits are available from the Angling Manager, Leisure Sport, RMC House, High Street, Feltham, Middx.

Ash Vale Lakes

Ash Vale Lakes are at Ash Vale, near Aldershot, Hants, and may be reached via the A3013. There are two small lakes of 7 and 4 acres, holding brown and rainbow trout. Fishing is by fly only, with a daily catch limit of 4 fish. Bank and boat fishing is available to members, who belong to one of two weekly divisions which exist to prevent overcrowding. Season: April 1 to September 30. Season permits available from Stillwater Fisheries Ltd, Yateley, Hants (tel: Yateley 873240).

Barn Elms Reservoirs

At Hammersmith, West London are the Barn Elms Reservoirs, reached from Hammersmith via Bridge Road.

This is a group of small, fairly shallow reservoirs, Nos 5 to 8 offering coarse and trout fishing. Species to be caught are roach, carp, perch and rainbow trout. The trout fishing on reservoir No 7 is by fly only. Reservoir No 8 fishing is by fly, spinning and bait. The other two reservoirs in the group are run as coarse fisheries. The waters are controlled by the Thames Water Authority. Day tickets are issued for trout and coarse fishing, although juniors under 16 must be accompanied by an adult. Permits from the bailiff on site, or in advance from TWA (Metropolitan Water Division), New River Head, Rosebery Avenue, London EC1.

Black Swan Lake

Dinton Pastures Fishery, Davis Street, Hurst, near Reading, is a noted trout water, reached via the M4, Winnersh exit (Junction 10), and the A329. There is a large car parking area. The attractively landscaped lake known as Black Swan takes its name from the exotic black swans that swim gracefully around the 75 acres water. With an average depth of 6ft to 8ft, the lake is well stocked with brown and rainbow trout, with a record rainbow of 9lb 8oz taken in 1975.

Fishing is by fly only, wet or dry, from the bank only, no wading. Recommended patterns are Butcher, Baby Doll, Black Muddler, Black Pennell, Black Nymph, Black Buzzer, Sweeney Todd, Alexandra, Zulu and Olive Nymph. The patterns should not be tied on hooks larger than a size 8. The catch limit is 5 fish of any size, and permits (day and season) are issued at the fishery hut. A full season permit entitles the angler to fish on any one day each week, and to bring up to five guests free of charge each season. Half-season permits entitle the holder to fish on any one day of each fortnight and to bring two guests during the season.

Season: April 15 to end of October. Fishing is from 9am to one hour after sunset.

Burghfield Fishery

A large area of gravel pit fishing controlled by Leisure Sport AC at Pingewood, Burghfield, Berks. Access is from Burghfield Road, via the A4.

The lakes hold good fish, and the top specimen must be the 3lb 9oz perch which was officially recorded. Alongside part of this lake runs a stretch of the Kennet, and this is also included on the permit. The latest recorded specimens from this large and irregularly shaped lake are tench 5½lb, roach 3lb 2¾oz and plenty of pike to 21lb. The Kennet has produced two barbel of 9lb 2oz apiece.

Season permits available from the Angling Manager, Leisure Sport, RMC House, High Street, Feltham, Middx.

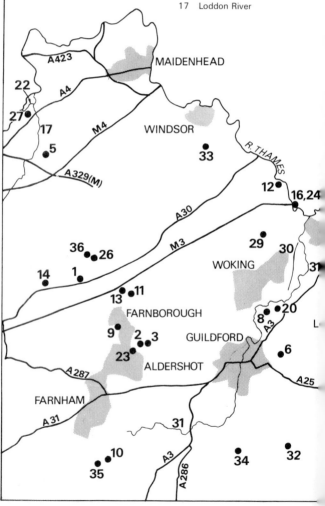

SOUTH WEST

1	A30 Pond	8	Cobbetts Lake
2	Ash Vale Fishery	9	Farnborough Lakes
3	Ash Vale Lakes	10	Frensham Ponds
4	Barn Elms	11	Frimley Lakes
5	Black Swan Lake	12	Greenham's Pit
6	Clandon Park	13	Hollybush Pits
7	Clapham Common	14	Horns Farm
		15	Lambeth Res.
		16	Littleton Lake
		17	Loddon River

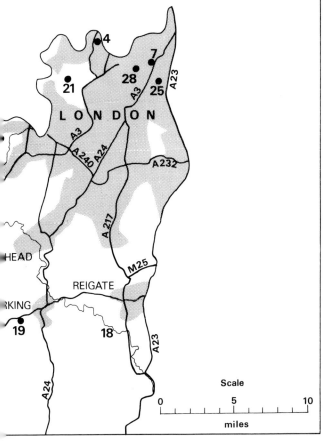

Clandon Park

Clandon Park Fishery is at West Clandon, Guildford, Surrey, with access from Clandon village off the A246 Guildford to Leatherhead road, about 30 miles from London.

Two man-made and carefully landscaped lakes of 8 acres and 1½ acres comprise this fishery in Clandon Park, and they are well stocked with brown and rainbow trout. The fishery record is a rainbow of 5lb 8oz.

Fishing is by fly only, and the catch limit is 6 fish per day, or 10 fish per week. There is restriction to dry fly only on the small lake. Season: April 1 to September 30. Fishery owner is the Rt Hon the Earl of Onslow. Season permits only from Messrs Weller Eggar, Cattle Market, Slyfield Green, Guildford, Surrey (tel: Guildford 73386).

Clapham Common

Clapham Common has two ponds that are often fished by local anglers. The most popular is the larger pond, and this holds a variety of coarse fish. Fishing is free, and in recent seasons tench, carp, roach and rudd have been caught.

Cobbetts Lake

At Send, near Woking, Surrey, is a coarse fishing lake that holds most varieties including bream, tench, roach, pike and perch. The fishing rights are held by Woking & District AC, and day tickets are issued in advance from the bailiff, Send Road, Old Woking, Surrey.

Criddell Lake

Criddell Lake is a landscaped reservoir at Ramsden, near Petersfield, Hants. It is reached via the A272, turning off left at Stroud. The water is about 54 miles from London.

This attractive 4 acres reservoir is well stocked with brown and rainbow trout. Fly only fishing, with a catch limit of 4 fish. Season: April 1 to October 15. The lake is controlled by Butser Turf Co. Ltd., 25 Portsmouth Road, Horndean, Hants (tel: Horndean 3242), and although no day tickets are available, there are alternative season ticket options. Applications should be addressed to the proprietors.

Farnborough Lakes

At Farnborough, Hants, there is a group of five well-stocked, ex-gravel pits, and these provide first-class coarse fishing. They are reached via the M3. The largest of the lakes is attractively studded with small islands, and the clean (often clear) waters hold a variety of species. Most of the banks are easily accessible and comfortable to fish from. Bankside vegetation offers cover to the angler stalking carp, which are frequently to be seen on the surface during summer months.

Floating crust cast well out from the bank catches some really big carp — over 20lb — and normal float-fishing and legering methods also take other species that inhabit the waters. Species: carp (over 30lb), tench, bream, roach, rudd, perch and pike. Controlling organization is Farnborough Angling Society; for annual permit apply to the secretary, J. Raison, 2 Park Road, Farnborough, Hants.

Farthings Lake

Set in a beautiful wooded valley is the 3 acre Farthings Lake, near Battle, Sussex. It is reached via the B2095, and access is by a small footpath opposite a track marked 'Millers Farm'.

The fishery is controlled by Water Recreation, 17 Clockhouse Lane, Ashford, Middlesex. The lake is well stocked, and the latest returns show fine catches, including bream to 6lb. One of the best catches to date was a haul of 190lb shared by two anglers.

A limited number of day tickets are available, with juniors and OAPs at reduced rates. Permits issued at local tackle shops, or from the bailiff at 23 Marley Rise, Battle.

Frensham Ponds

A great attraction for many anglers are the two lakes on Frensham Common, Surrey, both of which are well stocked with coarse fish, including tench, perch, carp, bream, roach and pike. These Frensham Ponds are set in picturesque surroundings on National Trust land, and the fishing rights held by Farnham AS.

There are two lakes known as the Large Pond and the Little Pond. Most attractive to anglers seems to be the Little Pond, which is not so small as its name suggests. It is about 60 acres in extent, and holds a fair head of fish. The nearby Large Pond, which is by far the bigger is noted for the specimens it has produced over the years.

The ponds are separated by the A287 road, may be reached from the A3, and are a little over 40 miles from London.

Day tickets are issued. Apply to Farnham AS secretary, R.T.Frost, 49 Cambridge Road East, Farnborough, Hants.

Frimley Lakes

A group of several small lakes at Frimley, near Farnborough, Hants, this fishery is reached from the A30 and then the A325. The nearest railway station is Frimley. The water is controlled by the Leisure Sport AC.

Fishing this series of lakes can be very interesting, with quality fish taken, including roach 2½lb, tench 7lb, perch 3lb, carp 20lb and crucian carp 3lb 6oz. For season permits only, apply to Angling Manager, Leisure Sport, RMC House, High Street, Feltham, Middx.

Greenhams' Pit

This gravel pit near Staines is particularly noted for its huge shoals of rudd. The fishing is controlled by the Taywood AS for members only.

Junior open matches held regularly on this water produce top weights of rudd exceeding 20lb - but senior club members frequently top 50lb.

Membership details from secretary E. Attwood, 86

Mansell Road, Greenford, Middx. This gravel pit fishery is reached via the Chertsey road from Staines.

Hollybush Pits

The three Hollybush gravel pits at Farnborough, Hants, owned by Redland Gravel Company, are included in that company's angling scheme. Day tickets are issued. The fishery is easily reached from London via the M3.

Horns Farm

Horns Farm is at Eversley, near Wokingham, Hants, with access from the A327, and is about 30 miles from London.

This is a 5 acre lake situated on a farm, and run on a 'put and take' basis. It is well stocked with brown and rainbow trout, with a 3 fish limit, all others taken to be paid for. Season: April 1 to September 30.

Day tickets, evenings and season permits are issued. Reduced rates for juniors and OAPs. Apply to Horns Farm, Lower Common, Eversley, Hants. (tel: Eversley 732076).

Kennet, River

The Kennet is the best of all the Thames' tributaries. Indeed it also ranks as one of the best English rivers, rich in fish of almost every species.

Its source is in the West Country, near Avebury, whence it flows through limestone country on its long journey to its confluence with the Thames at Reading, Berks.

Its upper reaches provide some of the best river trout fishing obtainable until, near Newbury in Berkshire, the river deepens and becomes a wonderful mixed fishery, as famous for its barbel, chub and roach as for its big trout. In this area the River Kennet and the Kennet and Avon Canal meet, and throughout much of its length the river is inseparable from the canal, the building of which in 1810 linked the Thames with the Bristol Avon. In places the two waterways, the canal and river, are one; in places they run almost side by side, and nowhere do they lose contact for long; because of this these waterways offer a

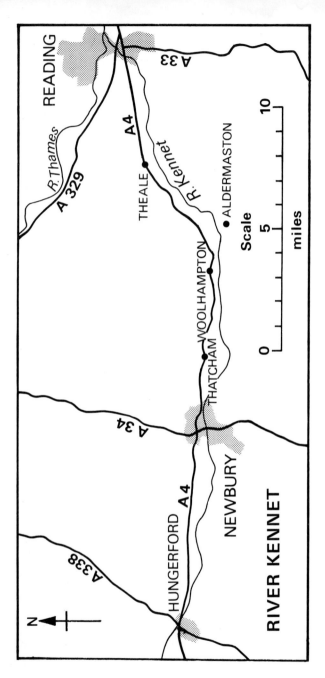

READING

R. Thames

A 329

A 33

A 4

THEALE

R. Kennet

• ALDERMASTON

Scale

WOOLHAMPTON

THATCHAM

A 34

NEWBURY

HUNGERFORD A 4

A 338

N

RIVER KENNET

0   5   10

miles

56

richness of fishing almost without equal. Chub, barbel, dace, roach, and trout grow to great size in the river, but the canal is also well known for its bream, pike and tench, as well as the first-named species.

From the point where the Kennet joins the Thames upstream to Huntley and Palmer's Bridge, Reading, there is some free fishing along the towing path. Most Kennet species — especially dace — are to be caught here.

There is some free fishing in the town centre, but from upstream of County Lock the fishing on the towing path side as far as Fobney is controlled by Reading and District AA. For membership details apply to F.W. Newman, 907a Oxford Road, Reading, Berks.

Along the Reading stretch the Kennet passes the CWS Factory, and the streamy swims here are noted for big barbel, bream and chub. Reading & District AA members have had barbel around the 10lb mark.

Fine roach and chub are taken from most swims of the waterway as it passes through pleasant meadow land to reach Fobney. In this area a barbel of over 14lb was caught some years ago, and even today there are a few double figure fish to be caught.

From Fobney Lock the Kennet and Avon Canal extends up to Burghfield, while the river runs separately around one meadow before again linking with the canal via a small weir pool.

Between Fobney and Burghfield there are three weir pools, and they hold some really big fish.

From Southcote to Burghfield the River Kennet runs separately, yet still close to the Kennet and Avon Canal. Fishing on this canal section is held by the Reading & District AA.

A prolific double bank stretch of this fine river is held by Leisure Sport AC for permit holders. With deep pools and fast shallows the river offers wonderful fishing for roach, dace, chub (5lb), and barbel with two fish over 9lb recorded. Fishing is by season permit, and includes a vast gravel pit lake adjacent to the river. Applications to the Angling Manager, Leisure Sport, RMC House, High Street, Feltham, Middx.

Upstream to Burghfield Bridge the Kennet, river and canal, flow as one to beyond Burghfield Lock is Reading & District AA fishery. Burghfield is a great fishing area, with 7lb chub recorded a few seasons back. This venue is easily reached from the M4, A4, and via Burghfield Road. Some may find it difficult to tell river from canal anywhere along this reed-fringed stretch, which extends across delightful meadows.

At Sulhamstead, once noted for 6lb chub, the fishing in the British Waterways Board stretch at Tyle Mill, is available on day tickets issued at the bailiff's cottage. Pleasant general fishing is to be had here.

Theale, situated alongside the A4 and close to the M4, is a particularly noted area for providing good sport with quality fish. In this area Reading & District AA permit holders have a length of canal fishing from Gaston Pound Lock up to Wide Mead Lock. The Association also holds the rights to an attractive river stretch that includes Cumbers Meadow. Excellent fishing for chub, roach, dace and barbel.

Considered by many local and London anglers to be the best fishing area of the Kennet nowadays is the Padworth stretch. Here the Reading & District AA and CALPAC have fishing for their respective members.

Access to the RDAA two miles' stretch is at Ufton Road Bridge, and at Padworth Mill.

CALPAC hold the rights to a short single bank length, and membership is available to those who apply to F.W. Newman, 907a Oxford Road, Reading, Berks.

Always a prolific section of the Kennet is that at Aldermaston, easily reached from the A4. In this area the Feltham PS has a fishery, noted particularly for extremely fine roach, and plenty of barbel. Fishing is available on annual permits issued with membership, on application to the club secretary, R. Sharman, 36 Sandy Way, Walton, Surrey.

Popular with many day visitors is the weir pool, and this holds a wide variety of species. Permits are issued at the Mill House for the short, but interesting piece of water at Aldermaston.

Upstream is another Reading & District AA fishery, and this is included in members' permits. No day tickets. R & DAA members also have the Woolhampton section, noted here for chub and roach, although most other species are to be caught. Access is via the swing bridge reached from the A4.

In the Thatcham area several clubs have private water. One particular fishery, noted for its barbel sport, is held by Taywood AS for members only. Details from the Taywood secretary, E. Attwood, 86 Mansell Road, Greenford, Middx. Thatcham AA have fishing, and it is worth applying to their secretary, K. Roberts, Grovelands, 212 Benham Hill, Newbury, Berks.

Upstream end of this reach at Colthrop is a fine weir pool, a lively backstream, and a flowing stretch of canal water strictly reserved for members of Reed AA.

In addition to quality chub (6lb), roach (2¾lb) and some fair barbel, are carp, and several double-figure sized specimens have been taken in recent seasons. There is opportunity for visiting clubs to fish with the Reed AA. members, and no one should miss the chance if the opportunity presents itself. The secretary of Reed AA is P. Blackwell, 12 Colthrop Cottages, Thatcham, Berks.

At Newbury there are ample opportunities, and it pays to enquire at the local tackle shop. But also in this prolific area three clubs hold fishing rights, for members only. Apply to the clubs' secretaries—Twickenham PS, Mrs. G. Etherington, 49 Muswell Park Crescent, Hounslow, Middx; Newbury AA, T.A. Collins, 43 Valley Road, Newbury, Berks; and Civil Service AS, W.J. Bayliss, 35 Limerston Street, Chelsea, London, SW10.

Lambeth Reservoir

Near West Molesey, Surrey, the Lambeth reservoir is reached via the B370 Walton to Hampton Court road.

Reservoirs Nos 2, 3 and 4 in this group are noted for excellent coarse fishing, with a record 3lb 14oz roach taken some years ago. The fishing rights on these TWA Reservoirs Nos 2 and 3 are held by the Civil Service AS, and on No 4 by the London AA. No day tickets issued, but associate membership of LAA is available on application. For Civil Service AS membership apply to the secretary, W.J. Bayliss, 35 Limerston Street, Chelsea, London SW10.

Littleton Lake

Near Chertsey, Surrey, is a reasonably large lake controlled by the Twickenham PS. The water holds a wide variety of coarse fish, including tench, bream, roach, carp and pike. Roach of 2lb, pike of 20lb, and bream of 6lb have been caught.

Matches held on this water have been won with bream catches, and generally the top bags have been taken on he swing-tip leger.

Day tickets are issued at the lakeside by a club bailiff. Membership of the club is open, and includes other waters. Details from Secretary, Mrs. Etherington, 49 Muswell Park Crescent, Hounslow, Middx.

The lake is situated close to the B375 Chertsey road, and adjacent to the Thames and Chertsey Bridge.

Loddon River

At the top end of this Thames tributary the Stratfield Saye Fishery has the fishing on a delightful stretch of the river, holding fine dace, chub and roach. There are permits available on application to the Estate Office, Stratfield Saye, Near Reading, Berks.

Reading & District AA members have a fine stretch of the river downstream of the bridge at Woodley — there are chub, roach, and dace to provide sport. For membership apply to F.W. Newman, 907a Oxford Road, Reading, Berks.

A long stretch of the Loddon at Arborfield is available on day ticket issued to visiting anglers by Farnham AC. The fishery holds a variety of species, including roach, chub, dace, bleak, gudgeon, perch and bream. The club also has a stretch of the river at Sindlesham Mill reserved for members only. Apply to J. Frost, 49 Cambridge Road East, Farnborough, Hants.

Also at Sindlesham the London AA has a small fishery suitable for individual anglers. This extends from a notice board just above Loddon Bridge to the first ditch — about 300 yards. This is easily reached via the A329. Fishing is for members only. Apply to H. Wilson, London AA, 183 Hoe Street, London E17.

At Sandford the Twyford & District FC have a fine

stretch, holding bream, roach, and dace upstream of the weir. The Twyford club also have a great deal of fishing along the west bank to St Patrick's Stream. This fishery is reserved for members only (secretary: D. Metcalfe, Millwood, 10 Ambleside Close, Woodley, Berks).

Leisure Sport AC has fishing on the Loddon, at Twyford, noted for the quality of its fish population, with particularly fine barbel and chub.

Permit holders have a single bank length from the ford to the railway bridge, and a double length north of the railway bridge. There is also a lake, between the car park and the river, that is fishable. Season permits are issued on application to the Angling Manager, Leisure Sport, RMC House, High Street, Feltham, Middx.

Mole, River

This Surrey river, a tributary of the Thames, holds a wide variety of species throughout its length. It has a fairly fast flow, weedy in places, and noted for chub. Large roach are at times taken, and even carp are caught occasionally.

The river enters the Thames by Hampton Court Bridge, and from there to Dorking the river is carefully preserved by a number of clubs.

In the Molesey area there are several odd lengths offering the chance of some free fishing, for barbel, pike, roach, dace, chub and occasional trout. Also in this area there is a privately held stretch fished by members of the Kingston Working Men's Club. Enquiries to F. Webley, 25 London Road, Kingston, Surrey.

Another Kingston club, known as the Rodbenders, has a section of the river at Hersham. Also in this area the Molesey Thamesiders have fishing. Excellent catches of mixed species are taken in club events. There are no day tickets, and fishing is by annual membership, application to Kingston Rodbenders, Miss C. Torpey, 41 Selsdone Close, Elmers Avenue, Surbiton, Surrey, or to Molesey Thamesiders.

Good fishing is to be had in the Esher area where Feltham PS have a private stretch. This water provides sport with chub, roach, dace, perch and gudgeon. For membership details apply to secretary, R. Sharman, 36

Sandy Way, Walton, Surrey.

Further upstream to Cobham CALPAC have the Norwood Farm water. This secluded stretch of the river is noted for producing fine catches of mixed species. There are no day tickets, but membership is open to those who apply to the membership secretary, F.W. Newman, 907a Oxford Road, Reading, Berks.

Also in the Cobham area the Thames Angling Group has an exclusive stretch, extending for about one mile. A wide variety of species includes chub, roach, dace, gudgeon and perch, plus a few bream, carp and trout. This is a permanently pegged match stretch, and reserved for members of Thames Angling. Further details from B. Evans, Thames Angling, 11 Feltham Road, Ashford, Middx.

The adjacent upstream section, holding several species, is controlled by the City of London PS — no day tickets. Membership of this club also includes other waters in Surrey. Details from the secretary, C. Lawrence, 8 Montgomery Avenue, Hinchley Wood, Esher, Surrey.

Further upstream a particularly attractive five miles stretch of this Surrey river is held by the local Cobham Court AC, for members only. Fine catches are made by individual anglers, and even the top weights of club matches often run into double figures. Cobham club secretary is D. Brewer, 29 Station Road, D'Abernon, Cobham, Surrey.

Access to most of the fisheries in the Esher and Cobham areas is fairly easy from the adjacent A3 London to Guildford road.

At Leatherhead, just south of the town, there is a narrow yet inviting section of the river open for day ticket fishing. Enquire at the local tackle shop for further details. The local Leatherhead & District AC also has a section of the Mole, at nearby Mickleham. Apply for permit details to R. Boychuck, 22 Poplar Avenue, Leatherhead, Surrey.

Fishing rights along much of the river in the Burford to Dorking area are held by the Dorking & District AC. The water here is shallower, much cleaner, though weedy in places, and a wide variety of species offer sport to members. Day tickets are not issued. Membership details from the club secretary, L. Such, 20 Pixham Lane, Dorking, Surrey.

The A24 road to the south coast crosses the Mole at Burford Bridge near Dorking and where the river runs at the foot of the hill.

The next stretch up is at Betchworth where the fishing is controlled by Carshalton & District AS (secretary: J. Geddimore, 17 Prestbury Crescent, Woodmansterne, Banstead, Surrey). Day tickets are not issued, but some season permits may be available.

Old Bury Hill Lake

This 12½ acre lake at Westcott, near Dorking, Surrey, is a noted coarse fishery situated about 24 miles from London. Easily reached from the A25 Dorking to Guildford road.

The lake, man-made over a hundred years ago, has become renowned for the excellence of its fish. It is attractively sited on a country estate, the banks are natural, and reed fringed in places.

With an average depth of about 5ft, the water holds a variety of species. Top specimens recorded are pike 30lb, carp 25lb, bream 9lb, tench 8lb and perch 3lb.

Fishing is from bank and boats, from 6am to sunset, weekdays — but boats required before 7.30am must be booked in advance. Weekend fishing is from sunrise to sunset.

Day tickets and season permits issued at the lakeside, with a half-price concession for juniors and OAPs. Further enquiries to G. Rowles, 'Lakeview', Old Bury Hill, Westcott, near Dorking, Surrey.

Papercourt Fishery

Two lakes located at Send, near Papercourt, Ripley, Surrey, which are noted for large catches of perch and tench. A few seasons ago the lakes produced total catches of up to 100lb of fish. The lakes also hold a variety of other species. Recorded specimens include bream of 9lb, tench 6½lb, perch 2½lb, roach 2½lb and pike of 23¾lb. The occasional chub and crucian carp are also taken.

The fishery is controlled by Leisure Sport AC, and it is reached from the A3, turning onto the B368, and access is from Send Lane. Fishing is by season permit available from the Angling Manager, Leisure Sport, RMC House, High Street, Feltham, Middx.

Pen Ponds

Richmond Park, in Surrey, has two lakes known as Pen Ponds, and these are shallow, usually very clear and fairly weedy. Popular with specimen hunters, these ponds hold a variety of fish, including big roach (some close on 2lb), a few perch, common carp, crucian carp, tench and pike.

The Pen Ponds are difficult waters to fish, and sport only comes to those who persevere. Season permits to fish these Royal Park ponds at Richmond are available from the Superintendent of Hampton Court and Bushey Park, Hampton, Middlesex.

St Patricks Stream

This Thames backstream is noted for barbel, chub, and various other species. The Leisure Sport AC has a single bank length at Twyford, near Reading, Berks. It is reached from the A4, turning into Loddon Drive for access to the fishery.

The barbel run to 7lb, and a fishery rule forbids keeping them in keepnets. Season permits only, on application to the Angling Manager, Leisure Sport, RMC House, High Street, Feltham, Middx.

Springlakes

Springlakes are on the A3013, between Farnborough and Ash. The three well-established, spring-fed lakes, landscaped, and with a total 25 acres, are stocked with brown and rainbow trout. Fishing is by fly only with a daily catch limit of 4 fish. Bank fishing only, no wading allowed. Season: April 1 to September 30. Season permits, limited to 75 rods, are available from Springlakes Ltd, The Gold, Aldershot, Hants (tel: Aldershot 20434).

Stratfield Saye Lake

Stratfield Saye Lake of some 5 acres, near Basingstoke, reached via the M4, turning off at Junction 11, south onto the A33.

This is a trout fishery, with fly fishing for brown and rainbows. The catch limit is four fish, and there is an eight rod limit on the water. Season: April 1 to October 31, 8am to dusk. Day tickets (8 rods only per day) bookable in advance from Bailiff, Fishery Bungalow, Stratfield Turgis, near Basingstoke (tel: Turgis Green 543).

Taywood Lakes

These are two adjacent lakes at Chertsey, Surrey, that are noted for coarse fishing. Both lakes, separated by the M3, hold pike over 20lb with a top fish of 32lb caught.

There are plenty of bream, with a fine 13-pounder recorded, and the waters also hold roach, tench, carp, perch, bleak, etc.

An annual pike fishing competition held on this fishery almost always produces a fish over 20lb, with a match-winning 28½ lb pike taken on float-fished livebait a few seasons ago.

The fishing is controlled by the Taywood AS, no day tickets. Membership details from the club secretary, E. Attwood, 86 Mansell Road, Greenford, Middx.

The lakes are situated close by Chertsey Lock, and access is via the riverside road off the B375 by Chertsey Bridge.

Theale Fishery

There are two lakes comprising the Leisure Sport Theale Fishery, and they are both noted for producing quality fish, including such specimens as bream 5½lb, tench 5½lb, roach 2lb and pike over 16lb. The fishery is situated at Theale, near Reading, Berks, and reached via the A4 and M4.

There are no day tickets, only season permits issued by the Angling Manager, Leisure Sport, RMC House, High Street, Feltham, Middx.

Tooting Common

On Tooting Bec Common is a pond which is a popular venue for local and South London anglers. The pond has provided good sport, with tench up to 6½lb, carp 11½lb, pike, roach and — a few seasons ago — a surprise golden carp of about 6lb. Fishing is free.

Tri-Lakes Fishery

This fishery consists of the 18 acres Dawny Lake, holding a wide variety of coarse fish.

The fishery is situated at Yateley, near Sandhurst, Surrey, and access is via the Sandhurst Road which is connected at either end by the A327 and A321. These roads are easily reached from the A30, and there is a large car park at the entrance to the fishery.

This attractive lake, fairly shallow and studded with many small islands, holds tench, roach, trout, common carp, crucian carp and big pike. There are no restrictions on bait or method, and the fishery is open all year round.

Colin Homewood, the fishery owner, issues day tickets and evening permits on the site.

Twyford Fishery

The Twyford fishery, a lake holding tench over 5lb, plus bream, roach, carp, pike and perch. is situated at Twyford, near Reading, Berks. The water may be reached via the A321, turning into the Park Lane and car park. There is also a stretch of the River Loddon included on the season permit, available on application to the Angling Manager, Leisure Sport, RMC House, High Street, Feltham, Middx.

Waggoners Wells

There are three lakes in the Waggoners Wells fishery, owned by the National Trust. The property is situated near Grayshott, Hindhead, Surrey. About 42 miles from London the fishery is reached via the A3, then east from Hindhead.

Two lakes are reserved for trout fishing, fly only, and the coarse lake holds mainly carp and tench. Day tickets are issued at the lakeside by the warden.

Wandsworth Common

There are two ponds on Wandsworth Common. They hold a mixture of coarse fish, including carp, roach, tench and pike, and the fishing is free.

Wey Farm Fishery

An attractive lake at Ottershaw, Surrey, comprises the Wey Farm Fishery. This 5 acres natural lake has an average depth of 4ft to 6ft, and is used exclusively for angling, offering sport with roach, rudd, perch, tench and carp. Fishery is controlled by Outdoor Water Recreation Ltd.

To reach the fishery from London head for Chertsey, and then take the A320 Woking road for about three miles. The entrance to the fishery is on the right. Look for a large sign 'Wey Farm Kennels & Cattery' at the main gate. Pass through the entrance and turn right, passing through another gate with a notice concerning the fishery. Obtain a fishing ticket at this point. Vehicles must be parked at the far end of this road.

The best catch recorded was a haul of 100 tench up to 3lb taken by three anglers in an evening session. The best specimen taken is a perch of 4lb.

Fishing times are from 6am to sunset, but day tickets (which must be obtained before commencing to fish) are not available locally before 8am. So for an early-morning start tickets must be obtained in advance, from local tackle dealers or from Tony Thurlow-Craig, 47 Clockhouse Lane, Ashford (tel: Ashford 51800). There are reduced rates for juniors and OAPs.

Tickets on the morning, after 8am, are available from the first house on the right immediately after passing through the fishery gate — ring the bell at the bottom of the garden and day tickets will be issued at this point. Season permits and club bookings on application to Tony Thurlow-Craig.

Wey Navigation

About 20 miles from London, and from the River Thames and Wey confluence at Weybridge, Surrey, the Wey Navigation Canal extends towards Godalming. This canal, reckoned to be the oldest in England, has been owned by the National Trust since 1964. From Weybridge through New Haw to Byfleet, a 7½ miles stretch of fishing, is controlled by the Wey Navigation Angling Amalgamation and bailiffs issue day tickets along the bank.

This is a most attractive waterway, generally shallow in places at about 4ft to 5ft with the occasional deep pool.

From Weybridge Lock the canal extends through New Haw, Byfleet, Pyrford, and Send to Guildford where it joins the old Godalming Navigation. Throughout most of its length the canal is heavily shaded by bankside trees and shrubs.

The canal is easy flowing and kept fairly clear of weeds by the passage of boats. Yet there is a good stock of fish, including roach, bream, chub, carp, bleak, gudgeon, tench, perch and pike. The biggest carp caught in recent seasons was a 20lb fish.

Roughly the middle of this venue can be found by locating the White Hart public house, situated close by New Haw Lock, and the road bridge carrying the A318. The fishable bank extends in both directions from the lock.

Wey, River

This Surrey river is noted for coarse fishing, with plenty of chub and dace, and there are trout in some areas. The river passes through some delightful countryside along its course from around Hindhead to Weybridge, where it enters the Thames. The water varies from fairly fast shallows to typical deep chub holes close in to the banks. At Weybridge, and for most of its length, the fishing is controlled by clubs.

Around Godalming the Wey is a fine river, with a good head of fish. Several miles of the river here is held by the local Godalming AC and some fair bags of mixed fish are weighed in the club's matches. Lone anglers seek the chub, and fish around 4lb are taken most seasons. The Godalming AC also holds the fishing rights at nearby Eashing at Farncombe, reached from the A3100 road.

Continuing its journey the Wey reaches Guildford, where the main species are chub, roach and dace. The local Guildford AC controls the fishing in this area and day tickets are issued.

CALPAC hold the fishing on the Stoke Park Farm Fishery. This is for members only, and membership is open to those who apply to the membership secretary, F.W. Newman, 907a Oxford Road, Reading, Berks.

Along the Woking and Send reaches, and a short Relief Channel section, the fishing is particularly noted for chub. There are a few really big bream to be encountered, and some shoals of quality roach. This fishery is held by the Woking & District AC, and for membership details apply to R. Hatcher, 80 Hill View Court, Guildford Road, Woking, Surrey.

Byfleet AA take over the fishing as the river continues its downstream journey. This is reserved for members only, and application should be made to L. Chapman, 43 Eden Grove Road, Byfleet, Surrey.

Downstream at Addlestone the Leisure Sport AC has two single bank lengths, and catches have included barbel to 4½lb. Reserved for members only, the fishery is located in Wey Manor Road, off the A318. Applications to the Angling Manager, Leisure Sport, RMC House, High Street, Feltham, Middx.

At Weybridge the river is joined by the Wey Navigation and joins the Thames at Wey Lock. But boat traffic in summer can be a hindrance to good angling. The Wey in this area holds most of the Thames species and Epsom AS has about half a mile of interesting fishing. Day tickets are not issued. Membership details from D.S. Copperwaite, 67 Ewell Park Way, Ewell, Surrey.

Willinghurst Trout Lakes

These lakes are at Shamley Green, near Guildford, Surrey. Turn east off the B2128 from Guildford about 1¼m south of Shamley Green at the 'Smithwood Common: Cranleigh School' sign. After 600 yards take the left hand fork, and after 300 yards then turn left into Willinghurst Drive.

Four small lakes totalling six acres, holding rainbow trout, with the best taken at 5lb 13oz. Fishing is by fly only with a catch limit of 5 fish.

Season April 1 to October 30, fishing from 9.30am to one hour after sunset. Day tickets and season permits issued from J. St. G. Syms, Willinghurst, Shamley Green, Guildford (tel: Cranleigh 2828).

Windsor Great Park

This Royal Park holds three lakes well stocked with coarse fish. The largest of the lakes is Virginia Water which has a length of about 2½ miles. The others are Obelisk Pond and Johnson's Pond.

Virginia Water has been fishing well in recent seasons, with fairly good catches of tench and bream of around 6lb. The water also holds big pike. Other species include perch, carp, roach and rudd.

Virginia Water is the most popular of the lakes, lies alongside the A30 road, and has a large car park close by. Fishing is by season permit, on application to Crown Estate Office, The Great Park Windsor, Berks.

Winkworth Trout Fishery

The fishery consists of two old established lakes at the Winkworth Arboretum, owned by the National Trust. The Winkworth fishery, situated near Godalming, Surrey, is about 33 miles from London. The two lakes, known as Upper and Lower, are stocked annually with brown and rainbow trout, and fishing is by fly only from a boat. Catch limit six fish.

Day tickets are issued in advance by the Secretary, J.A.H. McKean, The Thicketts, Hascombe, near Godalming (tel: Hascombe 218).

Wishanger Trout Fishery

This fishery consists of two lakes of about four acres, is situated at Churt, near Farnham, Surrey, and is reached by going west from the A287 Farnham to Hindhead road. It is about ½m south of Frensham.

The lakes are stocked periodically with rainbow trout, and fishing is by fly only. The season is from April 1 to September 30. No day tickets. Season and monthly permits from Farm Manager, Wishanger Farm, Wishanger Estate, Churt, Surrey (tel: Frensham 2408).

Yateley Fishery

A dozen attractive lakes split into two groups are known as Yateley No 1 and 2 fisheries, situated near Camberley, Surrey.

These waters hold a wide variety of fish, including common, mirror and crucian carp, tench, roach, rudd, pike and perch. These lakes have all been well stocked, and numerous tench over 5lb are taken.

Best recorded species are roach 2lb 5oz, rudd 1½lb, crucian carp 3½lb, tench 8¼lb, common carp 18½ln and pike 29¼lb. Pike over 20lb are fairly common. Night fishing is allowed on this fishery. Travel from London to Camberley via the A30, then take the A327 to Yately. There is a large car park.

The Yateley Fishery is controlled by the Leisure Sport AC, and fishing is by season permits issued on application to the Angling Manager, Leisure Sport, RMC House, High Street, Feltham, Middx.

Tackle dealers

Angler's Kiosk, Wokingham Road, Bracknell, Berks.
Angler's Shop, 167 Ferndale Road, Clapham, London SW4
   (tel: 274 5618)
Angling Plus, 62 Central Road, Worcester Park, Surrey
   (tel: 330 4892)
Angling and Sports Centre, 40 Guildford Street, Chertsey,
   Surrey (tel: Chertsey 62701)
H. Baylis, Sheerwater, Woking, Surrey (tel: Byfleet 46525)
Castle & Sons, 3 Elizabeth Parade, Yateley, Surrey (tel: Yateley
   874700)
The Creel, Station Road, Aldershot, Hants (tel: Aldershot
   20871)
Cupits, 24 Bridge Road, Cove, Farnborough, Hants
   (tel: Farnborough 42939)
Dells, 213 St. John's Hill, London SW11 (tel: 228 1320)

Epsom Tackle, 43 Waterloo Road, Epsom, Surrey (tel: Epsom 23881)

Fish & Tackle Centre, 94 Church Street, Croydon, Surrey (tel: 686 6792 ext. 2)

Gerry's of Wimbledon, 170-176 Wimbledon Broadway, London SW19 (tel: 542 7792 and 540 6773)

Guns & Tackle, 81 High Street, Whitton, Middx (tel: 898 3129)

Jeffrey & Son, 134 High Street, Guildford, Surrey (tel: Guildford 72297/8)

F. Johnson, 189 Ferndale Road, Brixton, London SW9 (tel: 733 1722)

King & Son, 3 South Street, Farnham, Surrey (tel: Farnham 6303)

Molesey Pets & Angling, 96-99 Walton Road, East Molesey, Surrey (tel: 979 9083)

Noel's Tackle, 314 Fernhill Road, Farnborough, Hants (tel: Camberley 32488)

Noel's Tackle, 37 London Road, Blackwater, Camberley, Surrey (tel: Camberley 33323)

Parade Pets and Angling, 80 High Street, Sandhurst, Camberley, Surrey (tel: Yateley 871452)

L. Probert, 17 Rise Road, Sunningdale, Berks (tel: Ascot 23699)

J. Raison, 2 Park Road, Farnborough, Hants (tel: Farnborough 43470)

Roberts Bros, 114 Carshalton Road, Sutton, Surrey (tel: 642 6222)

Ron's Tackle, 465 Upper Richmond Road West, East Sheen, Surrey (tel: 876 4897)

Stabler's, 350-352 Garratt Lane, Earlsfield, London SW18 (tel: 874 4683)

Tackle Ltd, 180 Outlands Drive, Weybridge, Surrey (tel: Weybridge 42675)

Tackle Up, 151-153 Ash Hill Road, Ash Vale, Surrey (tel: Aldershot 27828)

Thames Tackle, 243 Burlington Road, New Malden, Surrey (tel: 942 1215)

Walton Tackle, 166 Station Road, Addlestone, Surrey (tel: Weybridge 42528)

Western Tackle, 151 Fleet Road, Fleet, Hants (tel: Fleet 40666)

Wings 'n Fins, 705 London Road, North Cheam, Surrey (tel: 330 4787)

Wokingham Angling Supplies, 105 London Road, Wokingham, Berks (tel: Wokingham 787122)

Wood's Pets & Angling, 7 Old Mill Parade, Sandhurst, Surrey.

4
South East

All waters described in this section lie to the south of the River Thames and to the east of the M23/A23 roads.

Barcombe Lake

A reservoir of 40 acres, near Lewes, Sussex, with access via the Barcombe Mills Road off the A26.

This is a concrete reservoir stocked with brown and rainbow trout. It is fly fishing only with a daily catch limit of 3 fish, 12ins. and over. Season: April 15 to October 29. The fishing is controlled by the Ouse Angling & Preservation Society. Day tickets issued only to Society members. Applications to the club secretary, Dr. J. Cotton, Down End, Kingston Road, Lewes.

Beult River

This may be a little tributary of the Medway in Kent, but it certainly holds big fish. The best reaches of the Beult extend from Yalding, where it enters the Medway to Linton, about 30 miles from London.

Much of this fishery is held by the ACT Fisheries. A 4½ miles stretch of this great little river, with many secluded swims around Benover, is split into sections which are named in ascending order 'Jean', 'Elsie', 'Kitty', and 'Stella'. Chub of 6lb 10½oz, tench 6lb 5oz, roach 3lb 5¼oz and bream of 10lb are among the quality fish that have been caught from this ACT fishery. There are numerous other species in the river.

ACT Fisheries also have a further stretch about five miles up river at Staplehurst.

No day tickets, but season permits only by application to ACT Fisheries, 170 Sydenham Road, London SE26.

Nearly a mile long stretch of the river at Hunton is held by the Bromley & District AS. Further details from

SOUTH EAST

1 River Beult
2 Bough Beech
3 Brooklands Lake
4 Chiddingstone Castle
5 River Cray
6 Crystal Palace
7 Danson Park
8 Darenth Fishery
9 Keston Ponds
10 Larkfield Fishery
11 Leybourne Lakes
12 Lovehurst Manor
13 Lullingstone Lake
14 River Medway
15 Moat Farm
16 Mote Park Lake
17 Scarletts Lake
18 Sundridge Lakes
19 Sutton-at-Hone
20 River Teise
21 Weir Wood

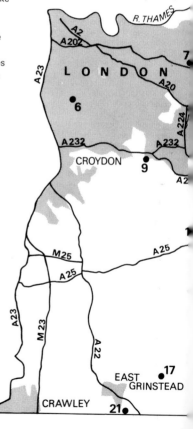

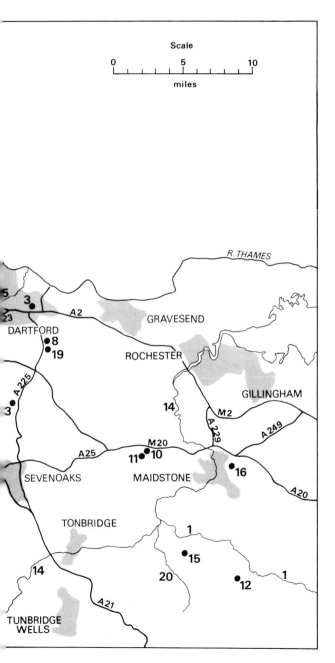

Scale

0   5   10

miles

R. THAMES

5

3

23

A2   GRAVESEND

DARTFORD

8

19   ROCHESTER

A225

3   GILLINGHAM

14   M2

A229   A249

A25   M20

11 10

16

SEVENOAKS   MAIDSTONE

A20

TONBRIDGE

1

15

14   20

12   1

A21

TUNBRIDGE
WELLS

M. Long, 40 Hacking Crescent, Beckenham, Kent (tel: 650 8468).

At Hunton Bridge, Chainhurst, the London AA have two fisheries on the river, known as Longfield Meadow and Pawley's Piece. This stretch of the river holds fine chub, roach and some bream.

The fisheries are reached from the A20 Maidstone Road, turning onto the A229 Road to Linton. The entrance is near Hunton Bridge.

The LAA also holds the fishing rights to a plum stretch of the river at Stile Bridge, Linton. This is particularly noted for its coarse fishing, a long single bank from the bridge, extending along the north bank. This fishery is also reached from the A20 and A22 to Linton and on for about one mile to Stile Bridge.

These LAA fisheries are restricted to members only, and membership details are available from the secretary, H.J. Wilson, London AA, 183 Hoe Street, London E17.

Boringwheel Fishery

This fishery consists of an attractive six acres of lakes near Nutley, Sussex, easily reached from the A22 East Grinstead to Eastbourne road.

Well stocked with brown and rainbow trout, the fishery has produced fish up to 8lb 12oz. Fishing is by fly only, and the season is from April 1 to September 30. A limited number of day tickets are issued by the owner, C. Impney, Boringwheel House, Cackle Street, near Nutley, Sussex (tel: Nutley 2629).

Bough Beech Reservoir

A landscaped reservoir of 275 acres, near Edenbridge, Kent, some 33 miles from London, access via the B269, 5½m west of Tonbridge. It is stocked periodically with brown and rainbow trout, and the fishing is by fly only from bank and boat. The season is May 1 to September 30. The reservoir is controlled by the East Surrey Water Co., London Road, Redhill. No day tickets. Full season permit and mid-week permits are issued – details from East Surrey Water Co.

Brooklands Lake

Dartford & District A & P S controls the fishing on the 20 acres Brooklands Lake, near Dartford, Kent. Big fish have been caught almost every season from this attractive water, and specimens include carp of 30lb, tench 6lb, bream and big roach. Society bailiffs issue day tickets. Dartford is some 17 miles from London, and reached from the A2.

Broombanks Lakes

There are three coarse fishing lakes at Broombanks, near Sittingbourne, Kent. Among the species to be caught are bream, roach, tench, carp, pike, perch and eels. Sittingbourne AC hold the fishing rights for members only, membership details from P.R. Smith, 72 Beaconsfield Road, Sttingbourne. The fishery is situated about 40 miles from London, and easily reached from the M2.

Chiddingstone Castle Lake

There is some fine coarse fishing in this lake. Most species are to be found here, bream being particularly good. In 1946 a British record bream of 13lb 8oz was caught from this water. Day tickets are issued.

Chiddingstone Castle Lake is situated about five miles east of Edenbridge, Kent.

Cray, River

A tributary of the Darent, rising near St Mary Cray and joining the Darent near Dartford. The water varies in depth from very shallow to about 8ft, and species to be caught are bream, tench, perch, roach, pike and gudgeon.

There used to be a good head of fish in this little Kent river, but much of the water is now diverted and the fishing is not what it once was, much of it being free now. The associated water of Ruxley Pits is the preserve of Orpington & District AC — details from the club secretary, R.Chappell, 163 Park Avenue, Orpington.

Crystal Palace

Situated in the grounds of Crystal Palace, South London, are two lakes, one of which is private fishing. The boating lake can be fished by visiting anglers on a day ticket issued by a park attendant. Season permits are also issued, with reductions for juniors and OAPs.

Both lakes are famous for large carp, up to 20lb. The lakes are also noted for big pike, a monster of 32lb having been caught a few years ago. But pike of 20lb have been caught since, and in addition bream to 5lb and roach of 2lb have been taken.

Danson Park Lake

This 20 acre park lake at Bexleyheath, Kent, is well stocked with coarse fish, and good nets of quality roach are taken. There are also bream and other species. Float fishing is the most successful method, and most of the usual baits will take fish. Fishing is allowed from Monday to Friday inclusive, and day and weekly tickets are issued (juniors free). Further details from Director of Parks and Recreation, 6 Gravel Hill, Bexleyheath, Kent.

Darenth Fishery

The Darenth Fishery consists of a group of five small lakes near Dartford, Kent. This fishery has the reputation of being one of the best carp fishing waters in Kent, with several fish around 20lb caught, the biggest recorded at 27lb 11oz. The large lake holds plenty of big bream, with a top fish of 8lb 13oz, roach over 2lb, tench 5lb and pike of 24lb 8oz, and a fine perch of 4lb 11oz.

To reach the fishery take the A2, turn south onto the A225, and then into Parsonage Lane to the car park. The waters are controlled by the Leisure Sport AC and available only to season permit holders. Apply to the Angling Manager, Leisure Sport, RMC House, High Street, Feltham, Middx.

Darwell

Darwell Reservoir is at Mountfield, near Battle, Sussex. This 180 acre reservoir is regularly stocked with brown and rainbow trout. Fly fishing from bank and boats; season: April 1 to October 29. The water is controlled by the Hastings Flyfishers (hon sec: 2 West Terrace, Eastbourne, Sussex, tel: Eastbourne 25211). Day tickets are issued, and boats cost extra. Advance bookings to the Bailiff, telephone Robertsbridge 880407. The best brown and rainbow trout have been in excess of 4lb and 8lb respectively.

Darwell lies to the west of the A21 Robertsbridge to Battle road (entrance at Tunstall Farm).

Hayton Manor

A natural lake of some 3½ acres at Hayton Manor Farm, Sellindge, Kent, is located about 1 mile off the A20 Maidstone Road. Controlled by the Mid-Kent Fly Fishers, this lake is well stocked with rainbow trout. The season extends from May 1 to October 31, and the fishing is by fly only. Season permits only are issued, on application to the secretary, E. Stratton, 6 Bell Meadow, Sutton Road, Maidstone, Kent (tel: Maidstone 61877).

Keston Ponds

These are two small ponds on Keston Common, near Bromley, Kent. There have been some good carp caught from time to time, including fish over 20lb. There are also tench up to 5lb, perch, roach and pike. The fishing is free.

Larkfield Fishery

Larkfield Fishery, near Maidstone, Kent is reached via the A20 or A25 to Wrotham Heath, turning onto the A228 and into Lunsford Lane for access to the fishery.

There are three lakes in this Leisure Sport AC fishery, and they all hold a variety of coarse fish. Among the specimens recorded are carp 28lb 11oz, bream 7½lb, eel 6lb 7oz, tench 5lb 2oz, perch 2lb 7oz, roach 2lb 12oz, chub 4lb 6oz and pike 27lb 6oz.

Night fishing is allowed on this venue, but no camping. No day tickets. Season permits from the Angling Manager, Leisure Sport, RMC House, High Street, Feltham, Middx.

Leybourne Lakes

These are four well stocked lakes controlled by the Alders A & P S. The fishery is at Leybourne, near Maidstone, and is reached by way of the A20. . Three of the lakes hold carp, roach, pike, etc., and the fourth lake is reserved exclusively for trout fishing. This attractive group of waters is for members only, and enquiries should go to the club secretary, D. Hook, 12 Larkspur Road, Stepstile Estate, East Malling, Kent.

Lovehurst Manor

An attractive stream-fed moat at Lovehurst Manor, Staplehurst, Kent, offers interesting trout fishing. The fishery holds wild brown trout, and is stocked with rainbows. Fishing is by fly only, and the season is from April 1 to October 15. It is controlled by the Mid-Kent Fly Fishers, and fishing is by season permits issued by the club secretary, E. Stratton, 6 Bell Meadow, Sutton Road, Maidstone, Kent (tel: Maidstone 61877).

The fishery is situated at Staplehurst, off the A229, about 8 miles south south east of Maidstone.

Lullingstone Lake

This 15 acre trout fishery is held by the Kingfishers APS for members only. The lake is fed by the River Darenth, and holds mainly rainbow trout with a few natural browns.

Fishing is by fly only. Annual membership also includes coarse fishing on other waters held by the club. Apply to the club secretary, P.D. Stewart, Heathfield House, Bourne Road, Crayford, Kent.

Medway, River

The River Medway is indeed one of the Londoner's rivers, and this is chiefly due to the fact that it is easily reached and provides interesting fishing.

The Medway rises near Forest Row and enters the sea at Sheerness. Throughout its reaches there are fine bream, roach, dace, chub and pike — plus a few other species, including the occasional trout.

Tonbridge, easily reached via the A21, is one of the most popular fishing areas with plenty of places to fish. Tonbridge & District A & PS control most of the fishing in this area, including the sports ground, the Town Lock section, and to Eldridges Lock. Day tickets are issued, and there is a fine section reserved for members only. Apply to Tonbridge & District A & PS, A. Wolfe, 59 Hunt Road, Tonbridge, Kent.

A towpath stretch downstream from Cannon's Bridge is available on day ticket. There is some free fishing here to around Yalding bridge.

Yalding is a popular venue, and the Central Association of London & Provincial Angling Clubs holds nearly a mile of bank, for members only. Apply to F.W. Newman, 907a, Oxford Road, Reading, Berks.

There is some excellent fishing for bream, roach, and dace along this reach of the Medway, particularly along a fine stretch of the river extending to Branbridges where the Civil Service AS have a fine fishery for members only. There is also some day ticket water along this reach.

Further day ticket fishing is available at Wateringbury, and at Barming. In this area there is some free fishing, and the Maidstone Victory Angling & Medway Preservation Society has a fine stretch, some on day tickets (secretary: B. Hayman, 26 Sutton Road, Maidstone, Kent). There are some fine bream, including 4-pounders.

At Maidstone the river is noted for its good head of roach and bream, some running to the 6lb mark, with shoals of dace and bleak making up the catches.

Fishing is free from the towpath bank from East Farleigh to Maidstone Bridge, and onwards to Allington Lock. Float fishing is the popular method, and access to the river is easy.

Moat Farm

The Mid-Kent Fly Fishers have a 2½ acre landscaped lake at Moat Farm, Collier Street, near Maidstone, Kent. This is a trout fishery stocked with rainbows, with a recorded best at 4½lb. The season is from April 1 to October 15, and the fishing is by fly only.

The fishery is reached from the A229, about seven miles from Maidstone. Fishing is by season permit only, obtainable from E. Stratton (secretary), 6 Bell Meadow, Sutton Road, Maidstone, Kent (tel: Maidstone 61877).

Mote Park Lake

One of the most popular stillwater coarse fisheries in Kent is the large lake at Mote Park, Maidstone. The lake holds a wide variety of species, and nets of mixed fish are weighed in in the occasional matches that are held. Visiting anglers have day ticket opportunities, and there are season permits for the regulars. OAPs and local residents qualify for a reduction in permit charge. Permits are issued by the Arts & Recreation Department, Colman House, King Street, Maidstone, and from local tackle shops.

Pippingford Lakes

A group of five lakes totalling some 30 acres at Nutley, Sussex, offers interesting coarse fishing. The lakes are stream fed and situated in the pleasant surroundings of Ashdown Forest.

Pippingford, originally a trout fishery, was opened for coarse fishing in 1957. The lakes have varying depths from shallow areas to 15 ft deep swims.

Stock includes 20lb plus carp, bream to 8 lb, tench, roach, rudd, pike, perch, golden orfe and big gudgeon.

A larger lake of some 28 acres that was once a 'hammer pond', will be included in the fishery for the 1978 season.

Day permits from the bailiff along the bank. Further details from owner Mr. A. Morriss, tel: 082 571 2205.

The fishery is reached via the A22 London to Eastbourne Road, and lies some four miles south of Forest Row.

The Pool at Pooh Corner Trout Fishery

This spring fed pool of 1½ acres, stocked with rainbow trout, is situated at Pooh Corner, about one mile from Rolvenden, Kent. Access is from the B2086, off the A28. Fishing is by fly only, using only one fly, of a conventional pattern. Day tickets are strictly limited, and available from L.Thomson, Pooh Corner, Rolvenden, Cranbrook, Kent (tel: Rolvenden 219).

Powdermill Reservoir

Powdermill Reservoir, also known as Great Sanders Reservoir, is at Sedlescombe, Sussex. Access is from Brede Road, off the A229 at Sedlescombe. It is a reservoir of 54 acres with natural banks, and stocked with brown and rainbow trout. Fly fishing only. Bank fishing is restricted to 10 rods, and there are 6 boats. The season is from April 1 to October 30, and the daily catch limit is 6 fish. Powdermill is controlled by the Hastings Flyfishers Club, 2 West Terrace, Eastbourne, Sussex (hon secretary, tel: Eastbourne 25211). Day tickets are issued, boats extra, all from the bailiff at the reservoir. For advance bookings telephone Sedlescombe 248.

Scarletts Lake

This small yet picturesque lake in a wooded valley is well stocked with coarse fish. The lake, of 3 acres, is at Hammerwood, near East Grinstead, Sussex, and is reached via a small private road off the A264.

The fishing is controlled by Water Recreation, 47 Clockhouse Lane, Ashford, Middlesex. Recorded specimens are carp 15lb, tench 6½lb, rudd 2lb and perch 2lb, and the fishing times are 6am to sunset.

Day tickets are available at the waterside, but season permits must be obtained from J. Jackson, Scarletts Farm, Furnace Lane, Cowden, Kent.

Sundridge Lakes

Sundridge Fishery, near Sevenoaks, Kent, is easily reached via the A25.

These are three lakes in the Darent Valley at Sundridge, and they are fed by the River Darent, once a noted trout stream. Well stocked with brown and rainbow trout, with a fishery record of 9lb 13oz rainbow, at least six trout over 9lb have been taken from Sundridge Lakes.

Fishing is by fly only, from bank and boats. The smaller shallow lake is under a floating line rule. Season: April 1 to October 31. The daily catch limit is five fish. Season permits only, from Rod and Line Ltd, 70-72 Loampit Vale, Lewisham, London SE13 (tel: 852 1421).

Artificial flies recommended for this water are Black & Peacock Spider, Grenadier and various Muddlers.

Sutton-at-Hone

A lake at Sutton-at-Hone, near Dartford, Kent, has produced 2lb roach, so it is well worth fishing. The fishery is reached via the A2 and A225, and access to the water is by Devon Road.

The fishery is controlled by Leisure Sport AC, and members have caught some quality fish, including tench to 5lb 12oz, chub of 4lb 6oz, carp to 18lb 4oz and pike of 23lb. Season permits only, on application to the Angling Manager, Leisure Sport, RMC House, High Street, Feltham, Middx.

Teise, River

This small Kentish river enters the Medway at Yalding. Trout and coarse fish. Upstream reaches strictly preserved by trout interests. At Lamberhurst the Royal Tunbridge Wells AS has a fine trout fishery, reserved for members and their guests. Details from C. Lupini, 27 Forest Road, Tunbridge Wells, Kent.

One of the best stretches of this attractive, small river, is at Goudhurst where the Teise Anglers and Owners Association holds the fishing on nearly six miles of the river to Marden. This long stretch is well stocked with brown and rainbow trout, and most of the fishery is restricted to fly only. Day tickets are not issued, and season permits on application to D. Cavey, 49 All Saints Road, Hawkhurst, Kent.

At Laddingford, near Yalding, the Mileham Farm fishery, trout and coarse fishing, is held by the London AA, for members only. The Association also holds the fishing on Manor Farm, with good chub, roach, dace and some trout. The upstream section, known as the Moss Farm Fishery, is also held by the LAA.

Access to these London AA fisheries is by the A20 Maidstone road. Turn onto the Teston Road, and follow the A26 into Yalding, then by B2162 towards Benover. The Teise fisheries are for LAA members — details of membership from the secretary, H.J. Wilson, London AA, 183 Hoe Street, London E17.

Tenterden Fishery

A small landscaped reservoir holding rainbow trout up to 5lb, situated at Tenterden, Kent, and reached via the A28. The season runs from April 1 to October 31, fishing is by fly only, and multi-hook lines are not allowed. Catch limit is two fish per day. Day and evening permits are available from B. Evan (owner), Coombe Farm, Tenterden (tel: Tenterden 3201).

Weir Wood Reservoir

Weir Wood Reservoir, at Forest Row, near East Grinstead, Sussex, some 33 miles from London, has always been recognized by trout anglers as the Londoners' Reservoir. Ideally situated on the edge of Ashdown Forest, the reservoir is reached by the A22. The reservoir entrance is 2½ miles from the railway station at Forest Row.

This attractive reservoir, of some 250 acres, was formed by damming the upper Medway. It was first stocked with rainbow and brown trout in 1955, and is stocked annually with several thousand fish. This popular trout water offers fishing by fly only, from bank and boats, from sunrise to one hour after sunset. Season: April 1 to September 30.

The daily catch limit for the water is six trout, of a minimum 12 inches in length. It is controlled by the Southern Water Authority, Guildbourne House, Worthing, Sussex. Day tickets and evening permits, after

4.30pm, are issued at the reservoir fishing lodge. Juniors under 14 years must be accompanied by an adult. For advance bookings telephone Forest Row 2731.

Wilding Farm Fishery

A 3 acre landscaped reservoir at Chailey, Sussex, comprises the Wilding Farm trout fishery. The lake is stocked periodically with brown and rainbow trout, and fishing is by fly only. The daily catch limit is four fish. Season: April 15 to October 1. Season permits only are issued, on application to J. Usborne, Wilding Farm, Chailey, Sussex. The fishery is reached from the A272, midway between Haywards Heath and Uckfield.

Tackle dealers

Angler's Complete Tackle Ltd, 170 Sydenham Road, London SE26 (tel: 778 4860)

Angler's Complete Tackle Ltd, 5 Tudor Parade, Well Hall Road, London SE9 (tel: 859 2901)

Angler's Corner, 16a Swingate Lane, Plumstead, London SE18 (tel: 854 3221)

Angling Suppliers, 304 Main Road, St. Mary Cray, Orpington, Kent

Angling Supplies, 53 High Street, South Norwood, London SE25

K. Briggs, 8 Loampit Hill, Lewisham, London SE13 (tel: 692 2565)

K. Brown, 9 Holmesdale Road, Bromley, Kent (tel: 460 5809)

Dawson's, 1 Chatterton Road, Bromley, Kent (tel: 460 7689)

J. Doust, Maidstone Road, Rainham, Kent

The Friendly Fisherman, 78 Camden Road, Tunbridge Wells, Kent (tel: Tunbridge Wells 28677)

GKM Tackle, 3 Parkside Parade, Northend Road, Dartford, Kent (tel: Crayford 529146)

Greenfield's, 4-5 Bridge Street, Canterbury, Kent (tel: Canterbury 62638)

Johnson's, 1577-87 London Road, Norbury, London SE16 (tel: 764 9711)

Keane's, 65 Bloomfield Road, London SE18 (tel: 854 1731)

Matchman Tackle, 64 Nunhead Lane, London SE15 (tel: 639 9078)

Medway Tackle, 103 Shipbourne Road, Tonbridge, Kent (tel: Tonbridge 355127)

G.W. Palmer, 19 & 21 Masons Hill, Bromley, Kent (tel: 460 4456)

Penge Angling, 7 Croydon Road, Penge, Kent (tel: 778 4652)

Rod & Line, 70-72 Loampit Vale, Lewisham, London SE13 (tel: 852 1421)

Specialist's Tackle, 125 Dulwich Road, Herne Hill, London SE24 (tel: 274 3927)

Toye's Tackle, 84 Broadway, Bexleyheath, Kent (tel: 303 4349)

I. Ward, 75 Masons Hill, Bromley, Kent (tel: 460 1906)

5
North East

All waters listed in this section lie to the north of the River Thames. The western limit is the River Lea, and the Lea itself is described in this section.

Abberton Reservoir

This is a vast reservoir of 1500 acres, near Colchester, Essex and reached via the A12.

It is noted for quality coarse fishing, from the bank only. Big bream around 10lb are often taken from this prolific water to stock other fisheries. Pike to 38½lb have also been caught.

Abberton is controlled by the Essex Water Co. Day tickets by advance booking only, applications to the Essex Water Co., Abberton Reservoir, Layer-de-la-Haye, near Colchester, Essex (tel: Layer-de-la-Haye 356) or to the Angling Centre, 31a St Botolphs Street, Colchester (tel: Colchester 5382).

Aquatels Fishery

The Aquatels Fishery, at Basildon, Essex, is always worth a visit. The fishery consists of one large lake of 23 acres for both coarse and trout fishing. The fishery record carp is around 32lb, and roach too are of good size, with a fishery record of 2lb 12oz. Other noteworthy specimens are perch 2lb 4oz, bream 10lb 8oz, tench 7lb, and crucian carp 2lb 12oz. To add variety there are rudd, grayling and, of course, the trout.

Day tickets are issued for coarse fishing, and for trout by fly fishing only. Reduced rates for juniors and OAPs. Coarse fishermen wishing to use two rods must pay an extra fee for the second rod.

Trout fishing is from a punt during the coarse season, and day ticket holders have a six fish limit, evening permits have a limit four fish. All tickets are available from the tackle shop backing on to the fishery — a mere 25 feet from the lakeside.

Further details from Aquatels, Cranes Farm Road, Basildon, Essex (tel: Basildon 27278).

Ardleigh

This natural reservoir of 130 acres, near Colchester, Essex, is reached via the A137 Colchester to Manningtree road.

It is noted for brown trout up to 9lb 11oz and rainbows. Fishing is by fly only, bank and boats, and the daily catch limit is 8 fish of a minimum 12 in. Season: March 26 to October 31.

This is a good early season reservoir, and recommended patterns include Ardleigh Nymph, Amber Nymph, Whisky Fly, Dunkeld, Black Lure, Baby Doll, Wickhams Fancy and Muddlers.

The water is controlled by Ardleigh Reservoir Committee who issue day tickets and full season permits. There are reduced rates for juniors under 18, and permits are available from the reservoir fishing lodge, or from the Fishery Officer, Ardleigh Treatment Works, Colchester (tel: Colchester 230642).

Basildon Park Lakes

There is coarse fishing available in Gloucester Park Lake, and in Lake Meadows, controlled by the Basildon (Essex) District Council. Day tickets are issued by park attendants.

Broxbourne Fishery

Broxbourne Fishery, at Broxbourne, Herts, is reached via the B194, and thence via Meadgate Lane. There are three large lakes and a small pool at the fishery, and all hold good fish. Recorded specimens are pike 26lb, carp 21¾lb, tench 2½lb, chub 5lb, bream 8lb 2oz, eels 4½lb and roach 2½lb. Night fishing is allowed.

The water is controlled by the Leisure Sport AC, and season permits are issued. Apply to the Angling Manager, Leisure Sport, RMC House, High Street, Feltham, Middx.

NORTH EAST

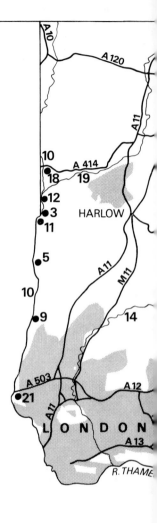

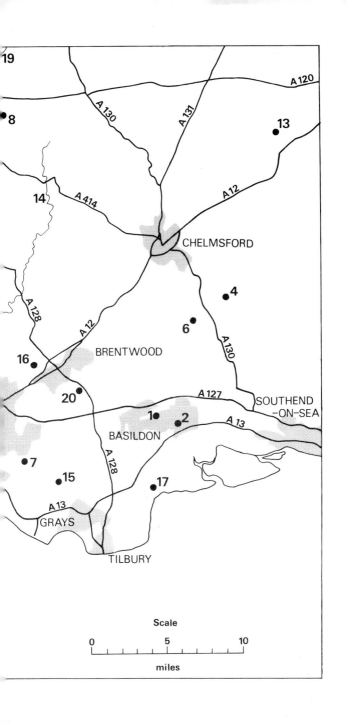

Bures Lake

London AA holds the fishing rights to Bures Lake, a popular coarse fishery reserved for members only. This water is limited to 30 rods per day, and members must sign in at the fishing entrance. Access is via Mill Lane from the A133 Colchester road. Membership is open to those who apply to the secretary, H.J. Wilson, London AA, 183 Hoe Street, London E17.

East Hanningfield Lake

East Hanningfield Lake, situated near Chelmsford, Essex, is a very old established water of about two acres. It is stocked with brown and rainbow trout. The season runs from March 19 to October 31, fishing permitted from 8am to half an hour after sunset. Fly only fishing available on day ticket and season permits from D. Benson, East Hanningfield Hall (tel: Chelmsford 400269).

Fishers Green

Fishers Green, a vast area of water at Waltham Abbey, is noted for good fishing. It is reached via the B194.

The lakes have fine bream, tench, roach and pike, and the biggest pike caught scaled 28lb. The fishery, which includes a stretch of the Lea, is controlled by Leisure Sport AC. Night fishing is not allowed, and no day tickets are issued, fishing being by season permit only, strictly limited, by application to the Angling Manager, Leisure Sport, RMC House, High Street, Feltham, Middx.

Foxearth Pits

There are three lakes near Glemsford, Suffolk, situated near the River Stour, and these are controlled by the London AA. The lakes, 18 acres, 14 acres and a smaller water, are all well stocked with coarse fish. Strictly members only. This fishery is reached via Chelmsford and then the A131 to Braintree, Sudbury and Long Melford, then the B1064 to Glemsford. Membership details from the secretary, H.J. Wilson, London AA, 183 Hoe Street, London E17.

Hanningfield

A reservoir of 900 acres at South Hanningfield, near Chelmsford, Essex, reached via the A130. This landscaped reservoir is well stocked with brown and rainbow trout. Fishing is by fly only, with a 6 fish daily catch limit. There is bank and boat fishing.

Hanningfield is controlled by the Essex Water Co, the season extends from May 1 to October 31, and there are no day tickets, season permits only from the Fishery Officer, Essex Water Co., Hanningfield Reservoir, South Hanningfield, Chelmsford.

Harwood Hall Lake

This is only a small lake, in park surroundings, but it holds really big bream which were introduced from Abberton Reservoir. Other species include tench, carp and roach.

The Harwood Hall lake fishery, in the area of the London Borough of Havering (Upminster), is controlled by South Essex Carp Fisheries, and day tickets are issued at the lakeside. Further details regarding season permits from T. Coster, 24 Finchley Road, Westcliff-on-Sea, Essex.

Hatfield Forest Lake

Hatfield Forest Lake (not to be confused with Hatfield in Hertfordshire) is situated near Takeley, about three miles from Bishop's Stortford, Essex, and is reached via the A120. This old established 4½ acres lake, owned by the National Trust, is less than 40 miles from London, and is noted for its tench fishing. Tench to around 4lb are frequently caught with the occasional 40-fish net. The best swims are reckoned to be along the dam section of the lake. This generally shallow lake also holds some fair pike, with fish of 20lb taken almost every season.

Day tickets, season permits and boat hire, from the Warden along the bank. Details, or advance bookings, from the Warden, Shellhouse, Hatfield Forest, Takeley, Bishop's Stortford (tel: Bishop's Stortford 870 447).

King George Reservoirs

Covering 420 acres, at Chingford, these waters may be reached via the A10. The two reservoirs are known as North and South, and hold a variety of coarse fish. The season is from June 16 to March 14. These Thames Water Authority reservoirs are controlled by the London AA, and there are no day tickets. An associate member permit is available on application to London AA, 183 Hoe Street, London E17.

Lea, River

The Londoner's other main river, apart from the Thames, is the Lea, and at weekends this accommodates many clubs and individuals. Much of the river has now been canalised along several lengths, with relief channels and diversions, but fishing on the Lea is now generally good.

In the Bow Creek area, near where the Lea joins the Thames, it is not considered as being worth fishing, yet roach, eels, chub and pike have been caught. The nearest worthwhile place for London anglers is at Tottenham, another not-so-popular fishing stretch, yet roach, bream, perch, chub, eels, gudgeon have been included in catches. Sport has been improving steadily.

Cooks Ferry has also improved considerably as an angling venue. Plenty of chub are there to be caught. Other species include roach, dace, bleak and gudgeon, and occasionally tench, bream and perch are taken. Recent seasons have seen this stretch develop into a favourite competition area, and the venue is easily reached via the North Circular Road.

There is another popular free fishing length at Edmonton, and at nearby Enfield is the New River Loop, for which day and season tickets are available from the Borough Treasurer, Civic Centre, Silver Street, Enfield, Middx.

Ponders End — again, here is a stretch which has improved much in recent seasons, with catches including roach, dace, chub, bream, and occasional big perch. A carp of 14lb 2oz was caught in 1951. The London Anglers Association released a hundred chub between 1½lb and 4lb into the area near the King George Reservoirs in 1971. The fishing in this area is on the Lea Diversion, and also on the Lea and Stort Navigation.

Cheshunt is another popular stretch of fishing where big catches of chub, roach, dace and bream have been taken. Other species which are keenly sought after are tench and perch, while occasional barbel have been caught.

Waltham Abbey is a favourite fishing place with large numbers of lone anglers. Its popularity makes it hard to catch fish. There is a wide variety of species including roach, dace, bream, perch pike, chub and tench. The best tench recorded during recent years scaled 5lb, with pike to 12lb. There are plenty of bleak to take the bait when no other fish will.

Waltham Abbey is an area where there is some free fishing water, and also a stretch where day tickets are issued along the bank by a bailiff.

Leisure Sport AC has the Fishers Green Fishery, which includes the Lea flood relief channel. This is noted for barbel with a top fish of 10lb 4oz recorded. Other specimens taken are chub to 5½lb, roach to 1½lb and bream 5lb.

The fishery is reached via the B194. This fishery is available on season permit from the Angling Manager, Leisure Sport, RMC House, High Street, Feltham, Middx.

At Wormley the London AA has the Kings Weir Fishery, and the Lea Navigation up to Aqueduct Lock. This Kings Weir area has provided anglers with some of the best sport, with good bags of quality fish, including one 80lb mixed haul in 1976. Most species are to be caught here. The main quarry of anglers are the bream, chub, barbel and roach. This is one of the best barbel fishing stretches on the Lea. Barbel are desirable quarry, and anglers are advised not to keep them in keepnets, but to revive each fish immediately after its capture and to ensure it is able to swim away.

There are day ticket opportunities, yet much of the fishing is controlled by the London AA, membership details from the secretary, London AA, 183 Hoe Street, London E17.

Dobbs Weir is another barbel area, with fish averaging around 4lb. In addition there are many of the usual species, including good roach and dace. Bream are worth fishing for because fish to 5lb are to be caught. A popular venue, with most of the best swims being taken early in the mornings, and at weekends there are always plenty of bleak here.

The other Lea fishery worthy of a visit is the Crown Fishery at Broxbourne. This comprises a long bank length extending below the bridge and upstream to Carthagena Lock. Day tickets are issued along the bank and the fishing is good for chub, tench, roach, dace, bleak and gudgeon. Big catches of fish have been made from the many attractive swims in the area. This is a popular competition venue which usually needs a big bag of fish to win. Numerous chub over 5lb have been taken. from along this reach and a 5½-pounder has been recorded. Day tickets are issued along the bank.

Hoddesdon has some deep swims, fringed with rushes, and these harbour some big shoals of great bream. The occasional tench or two may also be included in the day's catch, and perch to 3lb have been recorded.

London AA has water here, and Association bailiffs issue day tickets along the bank. The LAA also has the Rye House fishery, noted for its fishing, and day tickets are issued.

Near Fielde's Weir and Lock are a variety of good swims, all worth fishing, with pike to 15lb reported as having been taken. Other species include roach, dace, chub, perch and eels.

Fishing on a stretch of the Lea at Stanstead Abbots, Herts, is held by Leisure Sport AC. The water is available to season permit holders, on application to the Angling Manager, Leisure Sport, RMC House, High Street, Feltham, Middx.

St Margarets is another favourite venue visited every weekend by large numbers of anglers, who catch mainly roach, bream, dace, perch and the occasional trout. Also in certain swims tench are to be found, while a few pike have been taken too. Reports indicate that barbel have been caught from along this stretch. Throughout this reach there are hordes of bleak, the main quarry in some open competitions held here. There are ample day ticket fishing opportunities.

Ware is a favourite venue for anglers who fish for roach, dace and bream. In places it is reputed to hold trout. The pike and perch in this neighbourhood are small, although the eels which are at times caught here are quite big. Downstream of Ware the sheltered swims harbour bream over 4lb. The LAA has water in this area for members and associate members.

In the Hertford area it is mainly roach and dace fishing, but there are some chub, plus bream and sizeable perch. The deeper pools harbour the big chub.

Nazeing Pits

There are several Nazeing pits, covering about 50 acres, near Broxbourne, Herts. The fishing is controlled by Lynchnobite AS and reserved for members only.

Fishing is for a variety of species, with lots of small bream and some in the 3lb to 4lb class. There are big carp with fish up to 25lb taken, pike to 20lb, plus roach, tench and perch. Because the pits are so close to the Lea there are some chub and barbel.

Although some fine swims of about 12½ ft deep are situated close in to the bank, the more productive swims are said to be those of around 7ft to 8ft.

The fishery is reached via Nazeing Road, off the A10. There is a second entrance in Nursery Lane, Nazeing. Plenty of car parking areas. Apply to membership secretary, N. Hardington, 67 Norwood Avenue, Rush Green, Romford, Essex.

Netherhall Trout Fishery

A semi-landscaped gravel pit of about 6 acres, situated in Dobb's Weir Road, Hoddesdon, less than 18 miles from Central London and across the Lea Valley from the A10.

The water contains only rainbow trout, averaging around 2lb with bigger fish up to 6lb, and is restocked fortnightly through the season. The fishery rules stipulate fly only, no doubles, and no wading, which means fishing from the bank since there are no boats. The day limit is two brace.

Tickets are obtainable from the proprietor, Mr. A. Harris, Crown Fishery, Carthagena Lock, Broxbourne, Herts (tel: Hoddesdon 61048).

Rivenhall Lakes

There are several lakes and pits at Rivenhall, near Colchester, Essex, that are controlled by the Kelvedon & District AA. All are well stocked with a variety of coarse fish, including tench, bream, carp, roach and pike. No day tickets. Membership details from M. Frost, 1 Francis Road, Braintree, Essex.

Roding River

This Thames tributary rises near Dunmow and for the purpose of this guide becomes of interest when it flows through Ongar, Essex, where chub, roach, dace, pike and gudgeon are included in the catches. Most of the fishing on this river section is controlled by Ongar & District AS, and reserved for members. Further details from D. How, 85 Moulsham Lodge Estate, Chelmsford, Essex.

At Passingford Bridge, Woodford AS has some 2 miles, and season permits are issued on application to the club secretary, L. Lee, 2 Evanrigg Terrace, Woodford Green, Essex. A further section of the river upstream of the bridge is available on day tickets issued along the bank by a bailiff.

A section of the Roding between Loughton Bridge and Buckhurst Hill Bridge offers free fishing opportunity, with a variety of species including chub, roach, dace, pike, gudgeon and some bream.

South Essex Carp Fisheries

South Essex Carp Fisheries, at Ockendon, Essex, is a popular coarse fishing water some 18 miles out of London.

The fishery comprises three gravel pit lakes, named Shingle Lake, Square Lake and Long Lake. They were stocked a few years ago with big bream from Abberton Reservoir. Specimen bream have been caught, up to 12lb, and the lakes contain plenty of big common carp and crucian carp, plus tench, rudd and roach. The waters are suitable for float and leger fishing.

The fishery is open to any angler, who must first obtain a yearly member's card, and a bailiff then issues card-holders with a day ticket or a night fishing ticket. All members have free entry to the heaviest fish of the year competition.

Access to the fishery is easy, via the A127, turning onto the B186 to South Ockendon. Further details from Fishery Controller, Tom Coster, 24 Finchley Road, Westcliff-on-Sea, Essex.

South Weald Park Lakes

Essex County Council control the two lakes in South Weald Park, just north west of Brentwood. The lakes, of 8 acres and 2.3 acres, contain a wide variety of coarse fish — rudd, roach, tench, bream, perch, pike and gudgeon, to name but seven. Day tickets are only available for the larger lake. The smaller lake is set aside for the enjoyment of the more devoted of the fraternity, since only 150 yearly permits are issued for that water. Day tickets are available on the site.

Also at this location, across the road from the smaller of the park lakes, is another coarse fishing lake, but it is privately controlled and there are no day tickets.

Stanford-le-Hope

A two lake fishery at Stanford-le-Hope, Essex, is controlled by the Leisure Sport AC. It is reached from the A1014, by turning into Wharfe Road and then into the fishery car park.

This is considered a good roach fishing water, but there are also bream, carp, tench, etc. Season permits on application to the Angling Manager, Leisure Sport, RMC House, High Street, Feltham, Middx.

Stanstead Abbots

A three lake fishery at Stanstead Abbots, Hertfordshire, this group of ex-gravel pit lakes is reached by the A10 from London, turning onto the A414. The fishery entrance is in Marsh Lane. The fishery also includes a single bank length of the River Lea. In all lakes there are tench, bream and carp (the carp to 18lb). Season permits only issued, on application to the Angling Manager, Leisure Sport, RMC House, High Street, Feltham, Middx.

Stort, River

This tributary of the Lea offers interesting and varied coarse fishing. At Bishop's Stortford, Herts, the local Bishop's Stortford & District AC holds the fishing rights on several miles of the river to Spellbrook Lock, and at Harlow. Day tickets are available. For further information apply to the club secretary, C. Costema, 31 Thornbera Road, Bishop's Stortford, Herts.

Further downstream there is fishing from the towpath to the Iron Bridge. The length at Spellbrook is controlled by the London AA, and day tickets are available to local residents. The fishery on the Harlow Town Park stretch is controlled by the London AA, and the fishing for a variety of coarse fish (stocked by the LAA) is available to local residents on day tickets issued by the LAA.

The London AA has well stocked the stretch at Burnt Mill, with a large consignment of roach and bream, and the Association controls the fishing here as well as in the Town Park area. This fishery is for LAA members, and on day ticket for local residents.

At Roydon there is day ticket fishing on a stretch between the Station bridge and Mill bridge. Also in this area there is day ticket fishing down to the Lower Lock.

A fine two miles stretch of the Stort is controlled by the Lychnobite AS. This is the Temple Farm Fishery at Roydon, Essex. Day tickets are issued by a bailiff on the bank.

This coarse fishing river flows through Essex and Suffolk, and although much of it is private to clubs, it does offer plenty of fishing opportunities for London anglers. The river holds bream, roach, chub, dace, tench, pike, and perch, and some sea trout in tidal waters.

London AA holds the rights to a great deal of fishing on this river, with the upstream Clare Fishery in two sections comprising 1½ miles of single bank. Access to the Clare stretch of the river is made by gate opposite Cavendish Hall on the A1092, reached via Chelmsford. The London AA fishery is for members only, and membership is open to those who apply to the Secretary, H.J. Wilson, 183 Hoe Street, London E17.

At Glemsford, Suffolk, the LAA have two sections of river fishing, about two miles from Long Melford and reached from the A1092. The river widens as it approaches Sudbury, and here the local Sudbury & District AS (B. Roberts, Secretary, 45 Chelsworth Avenue, Great Cornard, Sudbury) have the rights to about six miles. Good roach and dace. Day tickets issued at the local tackle shop.

An almost double bank length of the river that consists of Pitmore Lock at Island, Henny Broad Meadow, and the Chauston Meadows are controlled by the London AA. Fishing along this fine stretch of the river is first class and it is reserved for members only. Apply to London AA Secretary. Access to this stretch is via the A12 Colchester road, then A133, taking the Henny Road, to Pitmore Lane.

The Lamarsh Broad Meadow fishery, near Bures, is controlled by the London AA, and the coarse fishing along the single bank length is excellent. For members only, apply to the London AA secretary. The fishery is reached via the A131, and the entrance is from Pitmore Lane.

Two sections of single bank fishing known as Secretaries Farm and High Pale Meadow offer day ticket fishing — permits issued by the bailiff at the water. The fishing is from the Essex bank, and is reached from the A133.

Also at Bures the London AA has Bridge Meadow,

Lower Meadow, Bures Millpool and the Mill Meadows. The river here has better depth, is tree-lined in places and holds bream, chub, roach and dace. To reach the fishery it is necessary to take the A12 to the Colchester roundabout, then take the A133 to Bures, entrance via Mill Lane. Also in this area the LAA has fishing on the Clicket Meadow and Staunch Meadows. Again, apply to the London AA secretary for membership.

Further downstream at Neyland the fishing is for a wider variety of fish, and species include chub, bream, dace, roach, tench, perch and pike. Much of the fishing is tied up by local organizations, and no day tickets are issued. A fine stretch of the river is held by the London AA, whose members have the Church Meadow stretch at Great Horkesley. Access is via the A134 Nayland Road, turning off to Little Horkesley and to the fishery.

At Dedham, Essex the fishing is held by the Angling section of Clovers Mill Ltd. The pool here is deep, and good for coarse fishing. Day tickets are not issued, but season permits are issued at the flour mills (Clovers Flour Mills, Dedham, Essex). Also along this stretch of the river the Kelvedon & District AA have useful fishing. Sport is reckoned to be good with chub, roach, dace, bream and pike. The fishery is reserved for members only. Enquiries to the club secretary, M. Frost, 1 Francis Road, Braintree, Essex.

Below Dedham is the noted Flatford Mill stretch near Manningtree, with the Essex Water Authority tidal water available for day ticket fishing. There is a further day ticket section upstream of the mill, with permits issued by a local club bailiff.

Thorndon Park Lake

This lake, also known as the Old Hall Lake, Thorndon Hall, is at the Thorndon country park at Ingrave, west of the A128 and about 3 miles south from Brentwood. It is a mixed fishery and day tickets are available on the site. There is another, recently restored, lake in the park, but this is strictly not for fishing and is kept as a nature reserve.

Walthamstow Reservoirs

These reservoirs, in north east London, are reached via the A10 and Ferry Lane, and are located about one mile from Tottenham.

Reservoirs Nos 1 to 5 provide coarse and trout fishing. Reservoir No. 4 (20 acres) is stocked with brown and rainbow trout. Fishing is by fly, float, and spinning. There is a daily catch limit of six fish, or four fish to part-day permit holders, and the season runs from March 15 to November 30.

The reservoirs open for coarse fishing are East and West Warwick, High and Low Maynard, and Nos. 1, 2, 3 and 5, and the Walthamstow group of waters is controlled by the Thames Water Authority. Day tickets are issued at the reservoirs. Juniors under 16 must be accompanied by an adult. Permits in advance from TWA (Metropolitan Water Division), New River Head, Roseberry Avenue, London EC1.

Tackle dealers

The Angling Centre, 31a St. Botolph's Street, Colchester, Essex (tel: Colchester 5382)

Avenue Tackle, 22a Woodford Avenue, Gants Hill, Ilford, Essex (tel: 550 7815)

The Bait Box, 40 King Street, Stanford-le-Hope, Essex (tel: Stanford-le-Hope 78821)

B&L Sports, Garron Lane, South Ockendon, Essex (tel: South Ockendon 6577)

L. Bowler, Merry Fiddlers Roundabout, Dagenham, Essex (tel: 592 3273)

Brainwoods, 57-59 Clarence Road, Grays, Essex (tel: 0375 4080)

Bromages, 666 Green Lane, Goodmayes, Essex (tel: 590 3421)

Brown's, 682 Romford Road, Manor Park, London E12 (tel: 478 0389)

Charlie's Fishing Tackle, 3 Nether Priors, Basildon, Essex (tel: Basildon 21854)

Duberry's, 19 Billett Lane, Hornchurch, Essex (tel: Hornchurch 49241)

Edco Sports, 136 North Street, Romford, Essex (tel: Romford 61181)

Godfrey's, 52 Moulsham Street, Chelmsford, Essex (tel: Chelmsford 84562)

R. Grief & Sons, 43 York Road, Ilford, Essex (tel: Ilford 2033)

Keith's Tackle, 209-211 North Street, Romford, Essex
   (tel: Romford 63370)

Lee's Fishing Tackle, 397 Roman Road, London E3 (tel: 980
   1130)

McDowell's, 39 High Street, Halstead, Essex (tel: Halstead 2321)

J. Mitchell, 410 Kingsland Road, Dalston, London E8 (tel: 254
   9333)

   Morris's, 37 Kings Road, Brentwood, Essex

Riley's, 322 High Street North, Manor Park, London E12
   (tel: 472 4604)

Robert's Tackle Shop, 192 Leytonstone Road, Stratford,
   London E15 (tel: 555 9372)

Simpson's of Turnford, Nunsbury Drive, Broxbourne, Herts
   (tel: Hoddesdon 68799)

T.H. Sowerbutts & Son Ltd, 151 Commercial Street, London E1
   (tel: 247 1724)

Walthamstow Tackle, 123 Fulbourne Road, London E17
   (tel: 527 1135)

Woodhall Pet Stores, 65 Wingletye Lane, Hornchurch, Essex
   (tel: Hornchurch 43419)

Index

*Printed in Great Britain at
the Anchor Press, Tiptree, Essex*